THE ANTI-ANTHROPOMORPHISMS
OF THE GREEK PENTATEUCH

PRINCETON ORIENTAL TEXTS

1. Usāmah's Memoirs. By Usāmah ibn-Munqidh. Edited by Philip K. Hitti.
2. Ottoman Statecraft: The Book of Counsel for Governors and Vezirs of Sari Mehmed Pasha, the Defterdar. Translated and edited by Walter L. Wright, Jr.
3. The Antiquities of South Arabia. Translated and edited by Nabih Amin Faris.
4. Illumination in Islamic Mysticism. Translated and edited by Edward Jabra Jurji.
5. Descriptive Catalog of the Garrett Collection of Arabic Manuscripts in the Princeton University Library. By Philip K. Hitti, Nabih Amin Faris, and Buṭrus 'Abd-al-Malik.
6. Descriptive Catalog of the Garrett Collection of Persian, Turkish, and Indic Manuscripts in the Princeton University Library. By Mohamad E. Moghadam and Yaḥya Armajani, under the supervision of Philip K. Hitti.
7. Al-Iklīl. By al-Ḥasan ibn-Aḥmad al-Hamdāni. Edited by Nabih Amin Faris.
8. Indus Valley Painted Pottery. By Richard F. S. Starr.
9. The Loves and Wars of Baal and Anat, and Other Poems of Ugarit. Translated and edited by Cyrus Gordon.
10. The Anti-Anthropomorphisms of the Greek Pentateuch. By Charles T. Fritsch.

THE
ANTI-ANTHROPOMORPHISMS
OF THE
GREEK PENTATEUCH

BY

CHARLES T. FRITSCH

Princeton

PRINCETON UNIVERSITY PRESS

1943

PREFACE

This study was presented originally to the Department of Oriental Languages and Literatures in Princeton University as a thesis for the Ph. D. degree. At the recommendation of my good friend and former teacher, Professor Philip K. Hitti, the work has been extensively revised and included in the Princeton Oriental Texts. To him I owe a debt of gratitude for his helpful suggestions and constant encouragement during the preparation of this book.

It is indeed a pleasure to thank Professor Henry S. Gehman, chairman of the Department of Biblical Literature in Princeton Theological Seminary, for his untiring interest in this work. He was the one who turned my thoughts to Old Testament studies in my student days at Princeton Seminary. He suggested this interesting topic for my doctoral dissertation, and he has been most generous in offering helpful criticisms during its preparation for the press. Words can scarcely express my heartfelt appreciation for his many kindnesses.

I am truly grateful to the Board of Trustees of Princeton Theological Seminary for the substantial aid they have contributed toward the defraying of publication costs. Also to those who have helped me with the proofreading and the indexing of the biblical references, especially to Dr. Bruce M. Metzger, my colleague on the Seminary faculty, I am deeply indebted.

Finally, it should be noted that all quotations from the American Standard Edition of the Revised Bible are given through the permission of the copyright owner, The International Council of Religious Education.

C. T. F.

Princeton, N. J.,
   April, 1943.

TABLE OF CONTENTS

THE ANTI-ANTHROPOMORPHISMS
OF THE GREEK PENTATEUCH

SYMBOLS AND ABBREVIATIONS

A	Codex Alexandrinus.
B	Codex Vaticanus.
D	Codex Cottonianus.
E	Codex Bodleianus.
F	Codex Ambrosianus.
M	Codex Coislinianus.
LXX	Septuagint (meaning the Pentateuch).
C-B	Chester Beatty Papyri.
M	Masoretic Text.
V	Vulgate.
'A	Aquila.
Σ	Symmachus.
Θ	Theodotion.
SH	Syro-Hexaplar.
Sam^H.	Samaritan Hebrew Pentateuch.
S	Syriac version or Peshitta.
B-D-B	Brown, Driver, Briggs (*Lexicon*).
G-B	Gesenius-Buhl (*Handwörterbuch*).
König	*Wörterbuch.*
TW	*Theologisches Wörterbuch* (Kittel, G.).
H-R	Hatch and Redpath (*Concordance to the Septuagint*).
HTR	*Harvard Theological Review.*
ICC	*International Critical Commentary.*
JAOS	*Journal of the American Oriental Society.*
JBL	*Journal of Biblical Literature.*
JQR	*Jewish Quarterly Review.*
ZA	*Zeitschrift für Assyriologie.*
ZDMG	*Zeitschrift der deutschen morgenländischen Gesellschaft.*
AV	*Authorized Version.*
JV	*Jewish Version.*
RV	*American Standard Version.*
"א	אלהים
"י	יהוה

INTRODUCTION

Ever since the beginning of the scientific investigation of the Greek Old Testament, scholars have noted that the translators sought to remove or moderate many of the human qualities and emotions attributed to God in the Hebrew Old Testament. Yet no one has assembled the examples, let alone classify them, for special study. It has been our purpose in this work to gather these instances from the Greek Pentateuch, to classify them in an orderly manner, and then to make comments on this material and draw definite conclusions.

This tendency in the Greek translations to avoid representations or conceptions of God under human form or with human attributes and emotions may well be called anti-anthropomorphic; and the actual examples themselves, anti-anthropomorphisms.

Furthermore, there are two senses in which the term anti-anthropomorphism is used in this investigation. First, in the technical, or narrow sense of the word, where it refers specifically to the avoidance of attributing human form to God. Included in this is also the denial to God of human emotions and passions; expressions of the latter kind are known as anti-anthropopathies. These examples are considered in the first two chapters.

Secondly, the term anti-anthropomorphism is used also in the general sense of removing or moderating any attribute, thought, or action connected with God which might lower his dignity, or degrade his honor or character. It is only as this term is extended to include these latter conceptions that it can be used as the title for this whole work.

Very little is said about this subject in the standard encyclopaedic and theological works. If mentioned at all, it is brought in under the treatment of anthropomorphisms, and then only a few standard examples are given. The scholars who have noted this anti-anthropomorphic tendency in the Greek Old Testament have concerned themselves almost entirely with the problem of its source, rather than with the phenomenon itself. As a result, the conclusions arrived at as to the origin of this tendency, based on no thorough study of the examples found in the Greek text, vary from those of men like Dähne[1] and

---

[1] Dähne, *Religions-Philosophie*, II, pp. 1-72.

Gförer,[2] who consider these anti-anthropomorphisms the result of
Philonic teachings and Alexandrian theosophy, to those of Frankel [3]
and Freudenthal,[4] who firmly hold that they are the result not of
Greek philosophical influence, but of the spiritual interpretations of
certain Biblical passages which grew up within Judaism itself.

In order to arrive at any conclusions in this matter, it is necessary
in the first place to have the data available for study and then to
subject each example to a critical, textual study, as well as to a
theological evaluation. This has been done here with the available
critical apparatus of the Hebrew and Greek texts, in comparison with
the Samaritan Pentateuch, Aquila, Symmachus and Theodotion. The
Syro-Hexaplar and Vulgate were consulted for critical problems. The
Authorized Version, the American Standard Version, the Jewish
Version and Luther's German translation have also been consulted,
as well as the commentaries upon the passages in question. The whole
question of the numerous anti-anthropomorphisms in the Targums
has not been dealt with in this work.

Before entering into the study of the anti-anthropomorphisms of
the Septuagint it is necessary to point out briefly the anthropomorphic
character of the Hebrew Old Testament, as well as its anti-anthropomorphic tendencies.

God, to the Hebrews, was a person, and the relationship between
God and man was of a personal character. The significant heritage
of Israel was that their God was the " God of Abraham, Isaac, and
Jacob," the God who had revealed himself to men as a person, and
who had personal dealings with all of his children. This personal
conception of God naturally led to frequent anthropomorphic expressions concerning the deity, some naturally more crude than others,
with the result that the Old Testament abounds with them. God
speaks, breathes, sees, hears; he walks in the garden; he sits in the
heavens; the earth is his footstool, and so on.

[2] Gförer, *Kritische Geschichte*, II, pp. 1-18.

[3] Frankel, *Vorstudien*, pp. 175 ff. and *Einfluss*, p. 30. In the latter work
the author lists the anti-anthropomorphisms according to the order of the
books in the Pentateuch, but the list is far from complete. As far as the
writer has been able to ascertain, no one since Frankel has dealt with this
subject by studying the examples themselves in a systematic and compre-
hensive way.

[4] Freudenthal, " Are there Traces of Greek Philosophy in the Septuagint? "
JQR, II, pp. 205-222.

On the other hand, there is an anti-anthropomorphic tendency in the Hebrew Old Testament which manifests itself in various ways. The words of the second commandment, in forbidding the making of graven images, show that God was not to be limited to any material or corporeal form (Ex. 20:4-6). No man could see God and live (Ex. 33: 20). It is said specifically in Num. 23:19 that God is not a man; and in Dt. 4:15, that the people saw no manner of form on the day that Jehovah spoke out of the fire on Horeb.

Then, too, besides the more naïve conception of God's appearing to man in human form, as in the Garden of Eden (Gen. 2), and in Gen. 18 and 32, there is what Eichrodt[5] calls "die Vergeistigung der Theophanie" (the spiritualization of the theophany) by means of such intermediaries as the angel of the Lord (Gen. 16:7; Num. 22:24, etc.), the glory of the Lord (Lev. 9:6, 23), the presence of the Lord (Dt. 4: 37), and the name of the Lord (Lev. 24: 11,16). The presence of these intermediaries in the Old Testament points to the fact that God was also considered to be a transcendent being, who revealed himself through other means than direct theophanies. Thus we find these two conceptions of God side by side throughout the whole Old Testament, and the paradoxical thing is that in those prophetical passages of the Old Testament which insist most firmly on the divine transcendence we find also the most unrestricted use of anthropomorphic language (cf. Is. 6: 1; Jer. 31: 32, 33; Ezek. 20: 33-36; Zech. 12: 4).

Finally, there must be mentioned the actual attempts in the Hebrew text to avoid anthropomorphisms. According to the documentary theory this tendency is present in some of the strata of the Pentateuch. E, for instance, is less anthropomorphic than J, for "the E author eliminated from his story all physical appearances of the deity to mortals, except to Moses alone."[6] Then, too, the priestly writer, called P, who recast the history of the patriarchal and Mosaic ages from a priestly and systematic point of view, presents a less anthropomorphic conception of God than either J or E. Descriptions of the deity's appearance are avoided, as well as anthropopathic expressions, "so that a purpose is here unmistakable."[7] Thus definite reactions against anthropomorphisms are visible in the composition of the Pentateuchal material itself.

---

[5] *Theologie*, II, pp. 5-18.

[6] Pfeiffer, *Introduction*, p. 174.   [7] Driver, *Introduction*, p. 129.

Although this does not come within the limits of this work, it should be noted that even though prophets, as well as poets, were making use of anthropomorphisms up to the latest times, they also guarded very zealously the transcendence of God. The champion of this cause was Ezekiel, who not only firmly believed in the unapproachable holiness of the transcendent deity, as is seen in his description of the ideal sanctuary (chapters 40-48), but who also in other passages used anti-anthropomorphic expressions to bring out this transcendent view of God. The following verses illustrate this last point:

> Ezek. 1: 26b, "and upon the likeness of the throne was a likeness as the appearance of a man upon it above."
> Ezek. 1: 28b, "This was the appearance of the likeness of the glory of Jehovah."
> Ezek. 8: 2, "Then I beheld, and, lo, a likeness as the appearance of fire; from the appearance of his loins and downward, fire; and from his loins and upward, as the appearance of brightness."
> Ezek. 8: 3a, "And he put forth the form of a hand."
> Ezek. 10: 1b, "as the appearance of the likeness of a throne."
> Ezek. 40: 3a, "and, behold, there was a man, whose appearance was like the appearance of brass."

Finally, in the Masoretic text itself according to the Masorah lists there are cases where certain words and expressions have been changed in order to avoid too gross or flagrant anthropomorphisms. Two examples from the Pentateuch are found in the list of eighteen emendations of the Sopherim, *Tiqqūnē Sōpherīm*, as quoted and discussed by Ginsburg in his *Introduction to the Hebrew Bible*, pp. 347-363. The first one is:

Gen. 18: 22   ואברהם עודנו עמד לפני י״

(but Abraham stood yet before Jehovah).

According to well-authenticated Masorah lists, this originally read:

ויהוה עודנו עמד לפני אברהם

(but Jehovah stood yet before Abraham),

but the text was altered. From the context itself, the original reading was certainly preferable, but, since "to stand before another" is sometimes used to denote a state of homage (Dt. 1: 38; 10: 8),

according to the lists of the Sopherim it was changed in order that
the deity would not appear to stand in such a relationship before
Abraham.

The other case is in Num. 11:15:

$$\text{וְאַל־אֶרְאֶה בְּרָעָתִי}$$

(and let me [Moses] not see my wretchedness).

Again there is strong traditional evidence from Masoretic sources that
this read originally:

$$\text{וְאַל־אֶרְאֶה בְּרָעָתְךָ}$$

(and let me not see thy [God's] evil),

i. e., the evil or punishment of God wherewith he would visit Israel.
It was changed, however, so say the lists of the Sopherim, to the
present reading to avoid ascribing evil to the Lord.

In both of these cases the Sam[H.] and the LXX agree with **M**,
which shows that these traditional changes were made at least in pre-
Septuagint times. It must be noted in these cases that well-attested
Jewish tradition is the only authority for these emendations. Nothing
can be proved, except the chronological fact that these changes must
have been made at least before Septuagint times.

One more class of examples may be included here. It has been
suggested [8] that the phrase:

$$\text{לִרְאוֹת אֶת־פְּנֵי י״}$$

(to appear before Jehovah),

was originally:

$$\text{לִרְאוֹת אֶת־פְּנֵי י״}$$

(to see the face of Jehovah);

in other words, the original reading of the verb was Qal; but because
of the objection felt to the expression "seeing the face of God," it was
changed into a Niphal. The passages in question are:

Ex. 23:15	וְלֹא־יֵרָאוּ פָנָי
Ex. 23:17	יֵרָאֶה כָּל־זְכוּרְךָ אֶל־פְּנֵי הָאָדֹן י״ (for אל read את)
Ex. 34:20	וְלֹא־יֵרָאוּ פָנָי

---

[8] Geiger, *Urschrift*, pp. 337-9.
Dillmann, *Exodus*, p. 276.
Driver, *Deuteronomy*, (*ICC*), p. 198, n.

Ex. 34:23	יראה כל־זכורך את־פני האדן י״
Ex. 34:24	לראות את־פני י״ אלהיך
Dt. 16:16	יראה כל־זכורך את־פני י״ אלהיך
	ולא יראה את־פני י״
Dt. 31:11	לראות את־פני י״ אלהיך

In all these cases the LXX has some form of the passive οφθηναι which means that the translators read the Niphal instead of the Qal; the possibility of such a change in the Hebrew must be recognized.[9]

---

[9] Two points may be added in favor of the changes in these passages. First, the cultic nature of all of these passages strongly suggests that the original idea was to come before the face of the deity with one's gifts on certain occasions, and see his face. (The actual expression " to see the face of God " occurs in Gen. 33:10.) Secondly, the usual prepositions with the Niphal of ראה ' to appear to some one ' are אל (Judges 13:10), and ל (Jer. 31:3).

CHAPTER I

ANTI-ANTHROPOMORPHISMS

In their attempt to spiritualize the conception of God, the translators of the Greek Old Testament avoided, to some extent, those representations which invested the deity with human form. It is in this strictly technical sense that the term anti-anthropomorphism is used in this chapter.

In Ex. 15:3, where God is called a man,

י״ איש מלחמה

(Jehovah is a man of war),

and in Num. 23:19, where the negative statement is made that,

לא איש אל

(God is not a man),

the LXX reads quite differently. In place of a concrete designation "a man of war," the Greek has a more abstract expression:

Κυριος συντριβων πολεμους

(Lord crushing wars);

and in the latter instance it has:

ουχ ως ανθρωπος ο θεος

(God is not as a man).[1]

The very idea of ascribing form to God is carefully avoided in the Greek of Num. 12:8:

ותמנת י״ יביט

(and the form of Jehovah shall he behold);

και την δοξαν Κυριου ειδεν

(and the glory of the Lord he saw).

---

[1] In the same verse, Num. 23:19, in a parallel construction with the words above, the Greek has "as" again:

ובן־אדם

(neither son of man);

ουδε ως υιος ανθρωπου

(nor as a son of man).

The face of God plays an important rôle in Hebrew Scriptures: from the naïve and concrete conception of פנים as the designation of the appearance of the deity (Gen. 32:30, 31 [31, 32]), to its own independent status as an *Erscheinungsform Gottes* (Dt. 4:37). In just a few cases has the LXX altered this conception.[2]

The term " Peniel " (Penuel), Gen. 32:30, 31 (31, 32), (the face of God), is translated in the Greek Ειδος θεου (appearance of divinity) and Ειδος του θεου (appearance of God), respectively.[3] According to the narrative, the spot was so named because Jacob " saw God face to face " (v. 31) and came out with his life. That ειδος means the same as פני in these instances cannot be held.[4] The LXX has purposely avoided the term " face " here in connection with God because פניאל is a place-name; but the expression " face to face " was taken over literally by the translators of the LXX, probably because they felt that as translators they could not tamper with the actual details of the narrative.

In Ex. 32:11 we read:

ויחל משה את־פני י" אלהיו

(and Moses besought Jehovah his God).

The root חלה in the Piel means " to make pleasant, to appease," and is used always with פנים (face), the idea being " to make the face of some one sweet or pleasant." [5] This strong anthropomorphism, although used metaphorically here in the Hebrew, has been avoided in the LXX by rendering it simply as:

και εδεηθη Μωυσης εναντι Κυριου του θεου

(and Moses made supplication before the Lord God).[6]

---

[2] The Seventy have translated פנים literally eighteen times in the Pentateuch when referring to God.

[3] In Judges 8:8 and I Kings 12:25 the word is transliterated φανουηλ.

[4] Cf. Delitzsch, *Genesis*, II, p. 206: " The name פניאל means, as the LXX translates it, ειδος θεου."

[5] Some suggest that the original meaning was " to stroke the face of some one," and thus " to placate " in that way, from the idea of stroking the idol in prayer. So, Bäntsch, *Exodus*, p. 271; Marti, *Geschichte*, p. 33 f. König in fact mentions the Arabic root خلّل (to rub) in connection with this Hebrew root, but there is no etymological connection between this root and خلّ (to be sweet) to which חלה is related.

[6] The omission of the possessive pronoun " his " in the phrase " his God " in the LXX makes the relationship between Moses and God less intimate. This

In three places in the Hebrew text פנים is used as a special form of God's appearance to his people, and in each case the LXX translated it by the intensive pronoun, αυτος :

Ex. 33 : 14

פני ילכו

(my presence shall go) ;

Αυτος προπορευσομαι

(I myself shall go before).

Ex. 33 : 15

אם־אין פניך הלכים

(if thy presence go not) ;

Ει μη αυτος συ πορευη

(unless thou thyself go).

Dt. 4 : 37

בפניו

(with his presence) ;

αυτος

(he himself).

may have been done purposely by the translators, although there is the strong possibility that it may have been an accidental oversight on their part, since the following word in the M text begins with a ו, viz., ויאמר, or they read the final ו as a ם, which would have been possible in the old Phoenician alphabet. In like manner the suffix referring to deity is dropped in the following passages of the LXX :

Ex. 23 : 27

אימתי

(my terror) ;

τον φοβον

(fear).

Dt. 32 : 10

עינו

(his eye) ;

οφθαλμου

(of an eye).

Ex. 15 : 7

קמיך

(those who rise up against thee) ;

τους υπεναντιους

(the enemy).

In none of these cases, however, can the omission be attributed to the misreading of the Hebrew text. The tendency to separate God from that which is physical as well as from that which is unbecoming to his majesty may have led to the Greek translation in these instances. Of course there are numerous passages in the LXX where the possessive suffix, referring to the deity, has been kept, viz., " my hand," Ex. 7 : 17, 6 : 8, Num. 14 : 30, etc.

פנים, originally " face," can mean here only the person himself insofar as he is present. Whether it means Jehovah himself or his Being as manifested in an angel (Is. 63 : 9) or as attached to the Ark is a debatable question.[7]   Whatever the Hebrew conception of this term may have been, the LXX has admirably reproduced its true meaning.[8]

The phrase בעיני י״ (in the eyes of Jehovah), or בעיני (in my eyes), where the pronominal element refers to Jehovah, is consistently translated into the Greek by words and phrases which avoid the mention of " eyes." Εναντιον, which is by far the most common, παρα and ενωπιον are the translations of this expression; also the preposition is omitted entirely in the Greek.[9] We may be quite certain that the Hebrew term had lost its literal significance, yet the original underlying anthropomorphic conception has been permanently eradicated

[7] Driver, *Exodus*, p. 361; Morgenstern, " Biblical Theophanies," *ZA*, XXV, p. 183.

[8] The phrase לפני and its variants (before, lit., to the face of) are consistently translated in the LXX by ενωπιον, εναντιον, απεναντι and εναντι (before). The Hebrew term had taken on prepositional value through semantic development, and the LXX correctly rendered the idea which the phrase expressed. Thus, with the exception of ενωπιον, which is rarely found as a translation of this expression, the LXX has avoided the literalism " to the face of " in its translation of this phrase. The examples are multitudinous, and can be cited at random in the texts.

[9] One example of each type follows:

Gen. 38 : 7   בעיני י״
                          (in the sight of Jehovah);
                           εναντιον Κυριου
                          (before the Lord).

Num. 11 : 15   בעיניך
                          (in thy sight);
                              παρα σοι
                          (with thee).

Ex. 33 : 17   בעיני
                          (in my sight);
                             ενωπιον μου
                          (before me).

Lev. 10 : 19   בעיני י״
                          (in the sight of Jehovah);
                                Κυριω
                          (to the Lord).

in the LXX with the exception of the comparatively few cases of
the use of ενωπιον.[10]

The "ears of God" and "to give ear" on the part of God were
also objectionable phrases, and so they too were changed by the Seventy.

Num. 11: 1   באזני י״

(in the ears of Jehovah);

εναντι Κυριου

(before the Lord).[11]

Dt. 1: 45   ולא האזין אליכם

(nor gave ear unto you);

ουδε προσεσχεν υμιν

(nor paid attention to you).

The word פה (mouth), when used of God, was carried over into
the Greek without any change.[12] Yet in Hebrew this word figuratively
came to mean "command," as that which came from the mouth; and
these instances, of which there are a goodly number, are translated in
the LXX by ρημα, προσταγμα, or φωνη.[13] This last Greek word is found
only in Numbers, which points to a different translator.

The term אף (nostril) came to mean "anger" in Hebrew by the
natural association of heavy breathing or snorting in connection with
this emotion. The Seventy accepted and translated the secondary
meaning of this word, using the words οργη and θυμος,[14] thus obscuring
the physical association. This is true in its use with God as well as
with man.

There are two places, however, where the Greek, by using the terms

---

[10] Three times in the LXX the word "eye" is translated literally when
referring to God.

[11] Num. 11: 18, exactly the same as Num. 11: 1 given in text above. In
Num. 14: 28 the Greek keeps εις τα ωτα μου.

[12] Cf. Num. 12: 8; Dt. 8: 3.

[13] Ex. 17: 1, etc. Greek ρημα for Hebrew פה. Num. 9: 18, etc. Greek
προσταγμα for Hebrew פה. Num. 3: 16, 39, 51; 4: 37, 41, 45, 49; 10: 13;
13: 4(3) Greek φωνη for Hebrew פה. Num. 20: 24 has substituted με for פי.
Num. 27: 14 has ρημα. The prepositions לפי, בפי, על־פי (according to) are
usually rendered by the simple prepositions κατα with the accusative (Gen.
43: 7), προς with the accusative (Lev. 25: 51) and επι with the dative
(Dt. 17: 6).

[14] Cf. Dt. 29: 20(19); 32: 22, *et passim.*

just noted, fails to bring out the original physical meaning of this word, which the Hebrew certainly meant to be expressed, because of the LXX's consistent adherence to a definite pattern of translation.   Thus two bold anthropomorphisms have been avoided in the LXX, and the meaning of the passages has been obscured.

Ex. 15:8   וברוח אפיך
(and with the blast of thy nostrils) ;

και δια του πνευματος του θυμου σου
(and through the wind [breath] of thy wrath).

Dt. 33:10   ישימו קטורה באפך
(they shall put incense before thee [in thy nostrils]) ;

επιθησουσιν θυμιαμα εν οργη σου
(they shall lay incense in thine anger).

In most cases the word יד (hand), when used in connection with God, is translated literally into the Greek.[15]   Two passages, however, show deliberate avoidance of the term:

Ex. 16:3   ביד י״
(by the hand of Jehovah) ;

υπο Κυριου
(by the Lord).

Ex. 24:11   ואל־אצילי בני ישראל לא שלח ידו
(and upon the nobles of the children of Israel he laid not his hand) ;

και των επιλεκτων του Ισραηλ ου διεφωνησεν ουδε εις
(and of the elect of Israel not one uttered a dissenting voice).

Another passage should be noted in this connection:

Ex. 14:31
וירא ישראל את־היד הגדלה אשר עשה י״ במצרים
(and Israel saw the great work which Jehovah did upon the Egyptians) ;

ιδεν δε Ισραηλ την χειρα την μεγαλην, α εποιησεν Κυριος τοις Αιγυπτιοις
(and Israel saw the great hand [the things], which the Lord had
      done to the Egyptians).

---

[15] Cf. Ex. 7:4; 9:3; Dt. 2:15; 4:34. This is true whether the word is literally used in the Hebrew, or figuratively.

The Hebrew here certainly intends יד to mean "display of strength, action," but the LXX literally translates it "hand." The following relative pronoun which refers to היד in the Hebrew was put in the plural neuter in the Greek. The Septuagint has translated the word "hand" literally, but it has brought out the figurative sense of the term by the use of a relative clause introduced by a neuter relative pronoun; thus the clause is in apposition with the idea inherent in την χειρα την μεγαλην.

. At this point it may be well to consider the expression in Dt. 33 : 27:

ומתחת זרעת עולם

(and underneath are the everlasting arms) ;

κaι υπο ισχυν βραχιονων αεναων

(and under [the] power of everlasting arms).[16]

In the Greek it appears as though the words ισχυν and βραχιονων are the translations of the same Hebrew word, זרעת, the one being figurative, the other literal. By introducing this abstract idea of power into the phrase the Greek has definitely weakened the anthropomorphism of the Hebrew.

Another very deliberate attempt to avoid a human conception of the deity is found in Ex. 15 : 10:

נשפת ברוחך

(thou didst blow with thy breath) ;

απεστειλας το πνευμα σου

(thou didst send forth thy breath).

It is true that the actual human activity is not avoided, but the Greek has definitely toned down the rather unbecoming action of blowing which is here associated with the deity in the Hebrew text.

In the technical sense of the term, the anti-anthropomorphisms in the Pentateuch of the LXX are disappointingly few. In most cases the translators literally rendered the anthropomorphisms of the Hebrew text. In regard to the translation of the Hebrew expres-

---

[16] Cf. Baudissin, *Kyrios*, I, p. 54, where he says that the article with ισχυν βραχιονων is purposely omitted to bring about an anti-anthropomorphism. It may also be a literalism, since the form זרעת is in the construct in Hebrew, and so necessarily without the article.

sions לפני, בעיני, פה and אף, however, it must be admitted that the translators sought to reproduce the meaning of these terms by their Greek equivalents without trying to express the literal meaning of the Hebrew original. The consistency with which this was done in these cases shows that the translators were governed not only by the desire to produce a faithful rendering of the original, but also to produce a version which reflected their knowledge of the Greek idiom and style as far as that was possible.

CHAPTER II

ANTI-ANTHROPOPATHIES

Human feelings as well as human form are attributed to God in the Hebrew Old Testament. God loves and rejoices; he hates and is jealous. He is subject to all of the passions and emotions of man. Now in the LXX some attempt has been made to avoid these anthropopathic conceptions, since they were considered objectionable in connection with God. The following examples illustrate this anti-anthropopathic tendency in the Greek Pentateuch.

The idea of repentance which is attributed to God several times throughout the Pentateuch is at variance with the omniscience of God, and so the Seventy consistently render the verb נחם (to repent) by some other meaning. Certainly if God knows everything from the beginning, he can never experience the feeling of repentance for any thing that he has done. The following examples illustrate this point:

Gen. 6:6   וינחם י״

(and it repented Jehovah);

$\epsilon\nu\epsilon\theta\nu\mu\eta\theta\eta$ o $\theta\epsilon$os

(God reflected, or was concerned).

Gen. 6:7   כי נחמתי

(for it repenteth me);

oτι $\epsilon\theta\nu\mu\omega\theta\eta\nu$

(for I have become angered).[1]

In two passages in Exodus the Greek translates the verb in a different way:

Ex. 32:12   והנחם על־הרעה

(and repent of the evil);

και ιλεως γενου επι τη κακια

(and be merciful in regard to the wickedness).

---

[1] M reads $\epsilon\nu\epsilon\theta\nu\mu\eta\theta\eta\nu$, but $\epsilon\theta\nu\mu\omega\theta\eta\nu$ is by far the better attested reading in A D E.

Ex. 32 : 14   וינחם י״ על־הרעה

(and Jehovah repented of the evil) ;

καὶ ἱλάσθη Κυριος

(and the Lord was moved with compassion).

Still another way of avoiding this term is found in Num. 23 : 19 :

ויתנחם

(that he should repent) ;

απειληθηναι

(to be threatened).[2]

In all of these cases the idea of repentance on the part of the deity
has been avoided, but the substitutions, with the exception of Num.
23 : 19, still retain anthropopathic color.[3]

Another good example of this anthropopathic tendency is found in
Gen. 6 : 6 :

ויתעצב אל־לבו

(and it grieved him at his heart) ;

καὶ διενοηθη

(and he thought it over).[4]

Then, too, the LXX attempts to avoid the ascription of anger to
God.

Gen. 18 : 30   אל־נא יחר לאדני ואדברה

(Oh, let not the Lord be angry, and I will speak) ;

Μη τι, κυριε, εαν λαλησω

(let it be nothing, O Lord, if I speak).

---

[2] Dt. 32 : 36   ועל־עבדיו יתנחם

(and repent himself for his servants) ;

καὶ επι τοις δουλοις αυτου παρακληθησεται

(and he shall be comforted for his servants).

Both of these meanings, " repent " and " be comforted," are justified according
to the Hebrew lexicons. The LXX has, perhaps deliberately, chosen the less
objectionable meaning in accord with its treatment of this verb.

[3] When used of a person, this verb נחם is translated by μεταμελει (it repents
[me]). Cf. Ex. 13 : 17.

[4] This verb עצב (to grieve) is found twice in the Pentateuch, with persons

The same expression occurs in Gen. 18:32 with the same Greek translation. There is a deliberate omission here of the verb חרה (to burn
[of anger]) because of its use in connection with God, but there are
numerous examples where it is retained under the same circumstances.[5]
Another verb קצף (to be wroth) is dealt with similarly in Lev. 10:6:

ועל כל־העדה יקצף

(and that he be [not] wroth with all the congregation);

και επι πασαν την συναγωγην εσται θυμος

(and wrath come [not] on the whole congregation).

The construction is made impersonal, and thus the feeling of wrath
is removed from God. But as with חרה this verb is also literally
translated when referring to God.[6]

In Num. 1:53 the idea of the wrath (of God) dwelling upon his
children is considerably toned down in the LXX:

ולא־יהיה קצף על־עדת בני ישראל

(that there be no wrath upon the congregation of the children of Israel);

ουκ εσται αμαρτημα εν υιοις Ισραηλ

(that there be no sin among the children of Israel).

Here the LXX purposely avoids the mention of the wrath (of God)
because of its anthropopathic association, and substitutes in its place
the idea of human sin.[7] But again there is no consistency, for in
other places the noun is found in the LXX in connection with God.[8]

In Dt. 3:26, the verb עבר (to be furious) is avoided in the LXX
by using an altogether different verb:

ויתעבר י"

(but Jehovah was furious);[9]

as subject. In both of these cases it is translated literally:

Gen. 45:5   λυπεω (grieve).

Gen. 34:7   κατανυσσομαι (be sorely pricked).

[5] E. g., Ex. 4:14; 22:24(23); Num. 11:1; 22:22; Dt. 6:15; 31:17; etc.
[6] Cf. Dt. 9:19.
[7] Cf. Bertram, "Der Begriff 'Religion' in der Septuagint" *ZDMG*, NF,
XII, p. 2.
[8] Cf. Num. 16:46 (17:11); 18:5; Dt. 29:28(27).
[9] This is the only occurrence of this verb in the Pentateuch.

και υπερειδεν Κυριος εμε

(but the Lord despised me).

In Ex. 31:17 we read:

שבת וינפש

(he rested and was refreshed);

κατεπαυσεν και επαυσατο

(he rested and ceased).

Here the Greek obviously avoids the idea of God's being refreshed by using a verb which is synonymous with the first one of the expression.

Finally, there is a case where fear, attributed to God, is omitted in the LXX.

Dt. 32:27   לולי כעס אויב אגור

(were it not that I feared the provocation of the enemy);

ει μη δι' οργην εχθρων

(had it not been for the wrath of enemies).

Thus it has been shown that, as with direct anti-anthropomorphisms, so with actual anti-anthropopathies, there is no consistent policy in the LXX. A problem remains in both of these realms. Why in the great majority of cases are the anthropomorphisms and anthropopathies carried over into the Greek without any change? The motive for this tendency to avoid the ascription of human form and feeling to God could not be consistently carried out. It evidently was not strong enough to overcome the anthropomorphisms of the Hebrew Scriptures, even though we are dealing with a Greek translation made in Alexandria. The Septuagint is after all only a translation, and is therefore subject to the same limitations of language as the original. No matter what theological or philosophical influences were present in the Judaism and Hellenism of the time of the Septuagint translation, they could be reflected merely as a tendency in a work whose main purpose was to bring the Hebrew Scriptures to the Greek-speaking Jews of Alexandria.

CHAPTER III

The Name of God Changed or Omitted

The examples in this and the following chapters are anti-anthropomorphisms in the general sense of the term, i. e., examples of the removing or moderating of those words or expressions which are unbecoming to, or disrespectful of, the deity. They have been classified according to certain general characteristics, and each chapter deals with one of these classifications which are described by the chapter heading. The first group deals with those cases where the name of God has been altered in some way in the Greek text.

In the Song of Moses, Dt. 32, God is several times called the "Rock," צוּר. This figure denotes the unchangeableness of Jehovah toward his people. The LXX consistently avoids this term by translating it by θεος. The passages to be cited are Dt. 32:4, 15, 18, 30 and 31. Even in v. 37, where the term is used of pagan gods, the Greek avoids it. What, it may be asked, was the reason for removing this idea of "rock" from the LXX text? Perhaps it was felt that the figure of God being a rock was too crude to carry over into the Greek translation. Or perhaps, as Bertram suggests, the reason was "religionsgeschichtliche,"[1] i. e., the fact that in Hellenistic religions "rock and stone are met with as symbol and seat of the deity, yea, even its embodiment" might lead to serious misunderstandings if it were disclosed that in the Hebrew Old Testament the true God was also called the "Rock." Whatever may have been the cause, the fact remains that by avoiding this forceful figure, a more refined conception of God was attained.

The name שׁדי (Almighty)[2] is found nine times in the Pentateuch. When by itself, it is translated by θεος (Num. 24:4, 16); אל שׁדי is translated by θεος μου, σου, or αυτων (Gen. 17:1; 28:3; 35:11; 43:14; 48:3; 49:25 [where read אל for את with Sam[H.], S]; Ex. 6:3). In the other parts of the Old Testament this term is translated mainly by παντοκρατωρ (Almighty) and ικανος (Sufficient).[3] The inconsistent

---

[1] Bertram, "Der Sprachschatz der Septuaginta und der des hebräischen Alten Testaments," *ZAW*, XVI, pp. 100-101.

[2] For the etymology of this word, see Albright, "The Names 'Shaddai' and 'Abram'," *JBL*, LIV, pp. 173-204.

[3] E. g., Job 5:17 (שׁדי: παντοκρατορος); Ruth 1:20 (שׁדי: ικανος). Cf.

way in which this word is treated in the Greek Old Testament shows that the translators had lost the clear meaning of the word, and so were content to reproduce it as best they could.[4]

Oehler,[5] however, makes the pointed distinction that "the LXX do not understand the expression in the Pentateuch, but it is correctly rendered by παντοκρατωρ in most passages of Job." Whether παντοκρατωρ be a correct translation or not, is not to be argued here, but it is true that there is a difference in the treatment of this word in the Pentateuch and the other books of the Greek Old Testament. To attribute this difference to the ignorance of the translators of the Pentateuch seems inconclusive since within a comparatively few years the translators of the rest of the Old Testament came across an explanation of the word. Is it not more logical to conclude that here again, as with צור above, there was a deliberate attempt to avoid the use of a term which for some reason or other was unbecoming to God?[6]

In Ex. 3:14 there is an obvious difference in the conception of God between the Hebrew and the Greek:

אהיה שלחני : אהיה אשר אהיה

(I am that I am, and, I am hath sent me);

εγω ειμι ο ων : ο ων απεσταλκεν με

(I am the one who is, and, the one who is sent me).

The rendering of the Hebrew אהיה by ὁ ὤν introduces a philosophic coloring entirely foreign to the Hebrew mind.[7] The difference consists simply in that the Hebrew conceives of God in a more personal way than the Greek. This does not imply that the Greek is altogether impersonal, for the masculine gender of the article with the participle is used; but the participial form is clearly less personal than the finite verb of the Hebrew.

This example throws a great deal of light on the whole problem of the development of the anti-anthropomorphic tendency from the

Zorrell, "Der Gottesname 'Šaddai' in den alten übersetzungen," *Biblica*, 8, pp. 215-219.

[4] So Eichrodt, *op. cit.*, I, pp. 87-88.

[5] *Theology*, p. 91.

[6] Perhaps the translators of the Pentateuch felt that a term like παντοκρατωρ was too closely associated with Hellenistic deities, and so had to be avoided. Cf. Pantokrator, in *Ausführliches Lexicon der Griechischen und Römischen Mythologie*, ed. Roscher, III, 1.

[7] Grether, *Name und Wort*, p. 6.

Hebrew through the LXX to Philo. Beyond a doubt the conception of God in the LXX is more spiritualized than that in the Hebrew Old Testament. He is farther removed from human affairs, and thus he is thought of in a more abstract way. He is no longer the אהיה of the Hebrews. On the other hand, the LXX carefully guards against a pure abstraction (τὸ ὄν) by making the participle masculine gender (ὁ ὤν). Thereby it *does not go so far as Philo*, who, besides ὁ ὤν, uses the term τὸ ὄν of pure abstraction for the deity.[8] The phrase ὁ ὤν therefore stands midway between the personal God of the Hebrew and the abstract conception of Philo, and that is exactly where the LXX stands chronologically in the development of this anti-anthropomorphic tendency.

Those passages are now to be noted in the LXX where ο θεος is written without the article for anti-anthropomorphic reasons. They are comparatively few in number, for ο θεος is the usual translation of אלהים, the one, true God. The indefinite form θεος was probably used by the translators to express a generic sense, " godhead," or " divinity," and then the adjectival idea, " divine." Thus, as the following examples show, the one, true God was disassociated from the physical factors involved.[9]

Gen. 1: 27 בצלם אלהים

(in the image of God);

κατ᾽ εικονα θεου

(according to an image of divinity, or, a divine image).[10]

Gen. 28: 17, 22 בית אלהים

(the house of God);

οικος θεου

(a house of divinity).

---

[8] Leisegang, *Indices*, pp. 226-27.

[9] Cf. Baudissin, *Kyrios*, I, pp. 50-56.

[10] Cf. Gen. 9: 6. The omission of the article with εικονα is probably a Hebraism, since the construct in the Hebrew has no article. The same explanation probably holds for the rest of the examples given above where the article is omitted in the Greek with the noun before the genitive. The Seventy may have purposely read כ (κατα) for ב (εν [so in Gn. 9: 6]) in order to soften the expression even more. It should be noted that in this verse בצלמו (in his image) is omitted in the LXX.

Gen. 32:30(31)   פניאל
(Peniel, or, the face of God);[11]

Ειδος θεου
(appearance of divinity, or, a divine appearance).

Gen. 33:10   פני א״
(the face of God);

προσωπον θεου
(face of divinity, or, a divine face).

Ex. 8:19(15)   אצבע א״
(the finger of God);

Δακτυλος θεου
(finger of divinity, or, divine finger).

Ex. 32:16   מעשה א״
(the work of God);

εργον θεου
(work of divinity, or, divine work).

Ex. 32:16   מכתב א״
(the writing of God);

γραφη θεου
(writing of divinity or, divine writing).

Num. 24:4, 16   אמרי־אל
(the words of God);

λογια θεου
(words of divinity, or, divine words).

Dt. 8:3   פי־י״
(the mouth of Jehovah);

στοματος θεου
(mouth [gen.] of divinity, or, divine mouth).

In the following examples ο θεος is found in the accusative without the article:

[11] In Gen. 32:31(32) the Greek has Ειδος του θεου.

כי ראיתי א״

Gen. 32:30(31)

(for I have seen God);

ιδον γαρ θεον

(for I have seen a Divine One [or, divinity]).

נתתיך א״

Ex. 7:1

(I have made thee God);

δεδωκα σε θεον

(I have set [made] thee a divine one [or, divinity]).

איש איש כי יקלל אלהיו

Lev. 24:15

(whosoever curseth his God);

Ανθρωπος ος εαν καταρασηται θεον

(whosoever curseth a Divine One [or, divinity]).[12]

Our last consideration in this chapter is the actual omission of the name of God from the Greek text. In most of these cases the omission can hardly be attributed to any spiritualizing tendency. In Gen. 22:2 the word המריה (Moriah) is translated την υψηλην (the high, the hilly), thus avoiding the last syllable of the name, which is יה, and which was probably understood as an abbreviation of יהוה. According to Siegfried, this is a deliberate attempt to set aside the name of Jehovah.[13] In II Chr. 3:1, where the name occurs again, the LXX transliterates it accurately (Αμορεια). This may be an example of the phenomenon which Frankel[14] suggests, namely, that the anti-anthropomorphic tendency is stronger in the Pentateuch than in the later books of the Greek Old Testament.

In Ex. 17:16 this same element יה is removed from a word in the Greek translation:

---

[12] The indefiniteness is emphasized also in the LXX by the omission of the pronominal suffix found in אלהיו. This omission may have been intentional on the part of the Greek translators, or they may have read the final ו as a ם, which would have been possible in the old Phoenician alphabet.

[13] Siegfried, *Philo*, p. 18. But cf. Sam.ᴴ המוראה; 'A την καταφανη Σ της οπτασιας; V visionis. Obviously there was consistent difficulty with this word. All the above versions agree, however, in connecting it with the root ראה, and in eradicating the latter half of the word. In Gen. 12:6 and Dt. 11:30 the word מורה (instructor) is rendered υψηλος.

[14] *Vorstudien*, pp. 175 and 230.

3

כי־יד על־כסיה

(Hebrew, because a hand upon the throne of the Lord; JV, "The
hand upon the throne of the Lord"); [15]

οτι εν χειρι κρυφαια

(because with a secret hand).

The expression "throne of Jehovah"—כסיה—has been altered in the
LXX to read "secret," as though from the root כסה (to cover, to
hide). Thus the "hand," which in the Hebrew must have belonged
to Moses, in the LXX becomes the property of Jehovah, but it is an
"invisible hand"; and the "throne of Jehovah" is removed entirely
from the passage.

Ex. 3:1   אל־הר הא׳ חרבה

(to the mountain of God, unto Horeb);

εις το ορος Χωρηβ

(to the mountain of Horeb).

This may be another intentional [16] omission to disassociate God from
a mountain, but Bäntsch [17] makes the suggestion that it was omitted
because the Greek translator took exception to the term "Gottesberg"
before the giving of the law.

Ex. 15:2   עזי וזמרת יה ויהי־לי לישועה

(Jehovah is my strength and song, and he is become my salvation);

βοηθος και σκεπαστης εγενετο μοι εις σωτηριαν

(he became my help and defence for safety).

The compressed translation of the Greek certainly tones down the
Hebrew exuberance and descriptive terminology of God, part of the
means of so doing being perhaps the omission of the name of Jehovah
itself. [18]

[15] In the text of the RV the translation of this phrase is "Jehovah hath
sworn" which is impossible from our present **M** text. In the margin, however,
the following translation is found: "Because there is a hand against the
throne of Jehovah," together with the translation of the Hebrew in substance
as given above.

[16] האלהים may have been left out by parablepsis, הר־חר״. In Num. 10:33
הר י״ is taken over entirely into the Greek, εκ του ορους Κυριου.

[17] *Exodus*, p. 19.

[18] But notice יה, ויהי, whereby the first two letters could easily be over
looked. The SamH. agrees with the LXX here.

The other three examples remaining are of no significance to our problem, but should be mentioned in this connection.

Lev. 6: 22 (15)   חק עולם לי״ כליל תקטר

(by a statute forever it shall be wholly burnt unto Jehovah);

νομος αιωνιος, απαν επιτελεσθησεται

(an everlasting ordinance, all shall be consumed).

This can be no deliberate omission here, for offerings are made by fire unto Jehovah again and again in the first part of Leviticus.

In Dt. 1: 8 and 16: 1 [19] the omission is due to the process of normalizing the Hebrew text in the Greek translation by using the same pronoun throughout a passage, rather than jumping from "Jehovah" to "I" or to "you," as is so frequently done in Deuteronomy.

---

[19] Dt. 1: 8   אשר נשבע י״

(which Jehovah swore);

ην ωμοσα

(which I swore).

Sam[H.] agrees with LXX here.

Dt. 16: 1   הוציאך י״ אלהיך

(Jehovah thy God brought thee forth);

εξηλθες

(thou didst come out).

But cf. Ex. 34: 18, where M has יצאת (thou camest out).

CHAPTER IV

Motion and Place Denied God

In the twelfth chapter of Exodus, in connection with the description
of the Passover, the verb פסח (to pass over) is used of Jehovah three
times, vv. 13, 23, 27. The root idea of this verb is probably "to hop ";
it then comes to mean " to pass over something quickly," " to pass
over without doing any harm."[1] The Greek has rendered this word
by σκεπαζω (to cover) in vv. 13 and 27, probably interpreting the
Hebrew to mean that if God passes over his people without doing
harm, he is covering, i. e., protecting or defending them. At any
rate, the Greek has avoided the idea of motion ascribed to God in
these two verses. In v. 23, however, the LXX retains the meaning
of the verb פסח by rendering it as παρελευσεται.[2] The examples follow:

Ex. 12 : 13 ופסחתי עלכם

(and I will pass over you) ;

κα ι σκεπασω υμας

(and I will cover you).

Ex. 12 : 23 ופסח י" על־הפתח

(and Jehovah will pass over the door) ;

και παρελευσεται Κυριος την θυραν

(and the Lord will pass by the door).

Ex. 12 : 27 אשר פסח

(who passed over) ;

ως εσκεπασεν

(since he covered).

The most interesting example of avoiding the ascription of motion
to God is found in those passages in Genesis where one is said to walk

---

[1] So G-B and König.

[2] In verses 12 and 23 the verb עבר (to pass over) is used with the deity
as subject. The idea of motion is not avoided in the Greek translation, which
is, in the respective verses, ελευσομαι (I will go), and παρελευσεται (he will
pass by).

either with God, or before him. In Gen. 5:22, 24, Enoch "walked with God," and in Gen. 6:9, Noah "walked with God"; in the remaining passages, Gen. 17:1, 24:40 and 48:15 the expression used is "walk before God." In the Hebrew, then, there was a distinction made between walking with God in pre-patriarchal times, and walking before God in patriarchal times. The latter expression denotes in a figurative way the idea of obedience to God throughout life, whereas the former expresses intimacy and close fellowship with God.

In the first group the Greek avoids the idea of man's being able to walk with God by using an altogether different expression, as the examples show:

Gen. 5:22   ויתהלך חנוך את־הא״
(and Enoch walked with God);

και ευηρεστησεν δε Ενωχ τω θεω
(and Enoch was well pleasing to God).

Gen. 5:24   ויתהלך חנוך את־הא״
(and Enoch walked with God);

και ευηρεστησεν Ενωχ τω θεω
(and Enoch was well pleasing to God).

Gen. 6:9   את־הא״ התהלך נח
(Noah walked with God);

τω θεω ευηρεστησεν Νωε
(Noah was well pleasing to God).

Thus, since Enoch and Noah are not allowed to walk with God in the LXX, it may be said that God does not walk with·them and so motion is denied God, at least in this particular connection.[3]

Although the other three cases cited above, where the expression is "to walk before," are not directly connected with the denial of motion to God, yet even here the Greek renders the verb הלך in the same way as above,[4] thus showing a consistent avoidance of this term "walking,"

---

[3] On the other hand, in Lev. 26:12 and Dt. 23:14(15), where God is spoken of as "walking" in the midst of his people, the word הלך is translated in the Greek by *ενπεριπατειν*. In Ex. 13:21, הלך = *ηγεομαι*. Cf. Ex. 23:23; 32:34; Num. 14:14.

[4] Gen. 17:1   אני־אל שדי התהלך לפני
(I am God Almighty; walk before me);

whether " with " or " before " God. The reason no doubt was to avoid the shocking idea that man could walk either with or before the deity. On the other hand, the idea of intimate fellowship implied by this expression in the Hebrew might easily suggest the idea of a " pleasing " relationship between God and these people.

Just as we have found instances in LXX where motion has been denied God, so we find even more examples of the denial of place to God.

Our first example is the verb יעד (to appoint), which in the Niphal means " to meet at an appointed place." By metathesis of the last two letters, forming Hebrew ידע (to know), the LXX, with one exception, consistently translates this verb by γνωσθησομαι (I shall be known).

Ex. 25:21(22)   ונועדתי לך שם
(and there I will meet with thee) ;

και γνωσθησομαι σοι εκειθεν
(and thence I will be known to thee).[5]

At first thought this change appears to be due to a misreading of the text, and if it occurred once or twice, it might be so considered. But when it is found in five out of six examples, there is reason to believe that the change was purposely made to avoid the idea that God and man could or would meet at an appointed place.

Εγω ειμι ο θεος σου· ευαρεστει εναντιον εμου
(I am thy God. Be well pleasing before me).

Gen. 24:40   י" אשר־התהלכתי לפניו
(Jehovah, before whom I walk) ;

Κυριος ο θεος, ω ευηρεστησα εναντιον αυτου
(the Lord God, before whom I was well pleasing).

Gen. 48:15   הא" אשר התהלכו אבתי
(the God before whom my fathers did walk) ;

ο θεος ω ευηρεστησαν οι πατερες μου εναντιον αυτου
(the God before whom my fathers were well pleasing).

[5] Identical passages are:

Ex. 29:42; 30:6, 36; Num. 17:4(19). In Ex. 29:43, the Greek renders the verb in question by ταξομαι (I will make an appointment or meet), which is the exception to the examples above. In Num. 14:35; 16:11; 27:3, when used of people, this verb is translated literally into the Greek, e. g., συναθροιζω (to gather together).

This idea of a deliberate alteration is confirmed by the fact that the expression אהל מועד (tent of meeting), i. e., where God meets with his people, is consistently rendered by the LXX σκηνη μαρτυριου (tent of witness).   In this case the Seventy derived the noun form from עוד (to bear witness). and not from יעד (to assign, to appoint), the correct root.   One example from the 116 occurrences in the Pentateuch will suffice to illustrate the point:

Ex. 33 : 7   ויקרא לו אהל מועד

(and he called it [the] tent of meeting) ;

κατ εκληθη σκηνη μαρτυριου

(and it was called [the] tent of testimony).

Another verb " to meet " (קרה) troubled the translators of the LXX.   Unlike יעד, this verb in the Niphal means " to meet " without pre-arrangement, usually with God as subject:

Ex. 3 : 18   נקרה עלינו

(he [Jehovah] met with us) ;

προσκεκληται ημας

(he has summoned us).[6]

The LXX has translated the verb in this way to avoid the anthropomorphism.[7]   So also in Ex. 5 : 3:

נקרא עלינו

(he [Jehovah] met with us) ;

προσκεκληται ημας

(he has summoned us).[8]

In Num. 23 : 3, 4 the verb קרה is translated into the Greek by φαινω ;[9] this is an obvious attempt to avoid the use of קרה.

[6] Sam[H.] נקרא   V vocavit.
Since the א and ה are quiescent in the last syllables of קרא (to call) and קרה (to meet), the two roots are pronounced the same.   Hence the reason for the easy shift from " meet " to " call " in the LXX.   This is reflected in Hebrew itself by the fact that קרא (to meet) exists as a parallel form of קרה.   Compare the example above (Ex. 5 : 3).

[7] So Bäntsch, *op. cit.*, p. 26.

[8] Sam[H.] נקרא   V vocavit.

[9] Sam[H.] has יקרא in v. 3; in v. 4, וימצא מלאך א" את בלעם ;   V has occurrere in both instances.

Num. 23:3   אולי יקרה י״ לקראתי

(peradventure Jehovah will come to meet me);

ει μοι φανειται ο θεος εν συναντησει

(if God appear to me in a meeting [i. e., face to face]).[10]

Num. 23:4   ויקר א״ אל־בלעם

(and God met Balaam);

και εφανη ο θεος τω Βαλααμ

(and God appeared to Balaam).

Once again, in the Balaam narrative, the LXX, by circumlocution, avoids the use of קרה.

Num. 23:15   ואנכי אקרה כה

(and I will meet [Jehovah] here);

εγω δε πορευσομαι επερωτησαι τον θεον

(and I will proceed to ask God).[11]

But in the following verse, Num. 23:16, the Greek literally translates the verb in question:

ויקר י״ אל־בלעם

(and Jehovah met Balaam);

και συνηντησεν ο θεος τω Βαλααμ

(and God met Balaam).[12]

Thus from these examples it is seen that, with two exceptions, the LXX has consistently avoided the idea of God's meeting with man, an idea which would not agree with the more spiritualized conception of God generally found in the Greek translation of the Old Testament.

Then, too, the idea of God's dwelling in some place is quite consistently avoided in the LXX. This is seen, for example, in the way the translators handled the verb שכן (to dwell).

---

[10] Actually nothing is gained here in the Greek since the phrase εν συναντησει is present. By this circumlocution, the Hebrew expression, however, is somewhat softened. Cf. Num. 11:23.

[11] Sam[H]. אקרא V obvius pergam (I will go to meet).

[12] Sam[H]. ויקרא מלאך י״ אל בלעם

Ex. 25 : 7(8) ושכנתי

(and I shall dwell) ;

κα οφθησομαι

(and I shall be seen).

Dt. 33 : 16 שכני סנה

(of him that dwelt in the bush) ;

τω οφθεντι εν τω βατω

(to him who appeared in the bush).[18]

This verb is also rendered quite frequently by the Greek verb επι-κληθηναι (to be invoked).

Ex. 29 : 45 ושכנתי

(and I will dwell) ;

και επικληθησομαι

(and I will be invoked).

Ex. 29 : 46 לשכני

(that I may dwell) ;

επικληθηναι

(to be invoked).

In the typical Deuteronomic expression, " the place which Jehovah your God shall choose, to cause his name to dwell there," the form לשכן (to dwell) is consistently rendered by επικληθηναι. One example will serve to illustrate this point:

Dt. 12 : 11 והיה המקום אשר יבחר

י״ אליהכם בו לשכך שמו שם

(then it shall be that to the place which Jehovah your God shall choose,
to cause his name to dwell there) ;

και εσται ο τοπος ον αν εκλεξηται Κυριος ο θεος σου επικληθηναι το ονομα
αυτου εκει

---

[18] Even the " glory of the Lord " does not " dwell " in Ex. 24 : 16:

וישכן כבוד י״

(and the glory of Jehovah abode) ;

και κατεβη η δοξα του θεου

(and the glory of God descended).

(and it shall be the place which the Lord your God shall choose that
his name be invoked there).[14]

It is true that "the name" and not Jehovah himself is "to dwell"
in these instances; but the name, as the expression of Jehovah's character and attributes, is so closely associated with him that the two
are practically identical. Thus, the expression itself in Hebrew is
anti-anthropomorphic in that the "name" is substituted for Jehovah
himself. The LXX simply carries the anti-anthropomorphism one
step farther by changing the verb.[15]

In the Book of Numbers, however, this verb is used twice with
Jehovah as subject, and in each case it is translated literally into the
Greek.

Num. 5:3   אשר אני שכן בתוכם

(in whose midst I dwell);

εν οις εγω καταγινομαι εν αυτοις

(among whom I dwell).

Num. 35:34

אשר אני שכן בתוכה כי אני י" שכן בתוך בני ישראל

(in the midst of which I dwell: for I, Jehovah, dwell in the midst
of the children of Israel);

εφ' ης εγω κατασκηνωσω εν υμιν. εγω γαρ ειμι Κυριος' κατασκηνων εν μεσω
των υιων Ισραηλ

(in which I shall dwell among you. For I am the Lord who dwells
in the midst of the children of Israel).

The literal rendering of שכן in the Greek of Numbers, as opposed to

---

[14] Other examples are in Dt. 12:5; 12:26 (in Greek only, probably to
correspond with the others); 14:22(23); 16:2, 6, 11; 26:2. In Dt. 12:21,
and 14:23(24), where לשום is substituted for לשכן, the Greek carries through
the same translation as in the others. In Dt. 16:15; 17:8; and 17:10, B,
following M and Sam[H]., omits the expression επικληθηναι το ονομα αυτου;
A F M and most of the minuscules have it.

[15] Dt. 33:12   ובין כתיפיו שכן
(and he dwelleth between his shoulders);

και ανα μεσον των ωμων αυτου κατεπαυσεν

(and he rested between his shoulders).

The verb שכן is not literally translated here, but the anthropomorphism is
by no means avoided in the LXX.

the translations of the term in Exodus and Deuteronomy just discussed, points to a different translator of Numbers from the other Books of the Pentateuch.[16] It appears that the expression was not ironed out by the Seventy in their final editorial work.

Finally a few isolated cases of this tendency must be noted.

Ex. 17: 6   הנני עמד לפניך שם

(behold, I will stand before thee there);

οδε εγω εστηκα εκει προ του σε

(here. [or, behold] I stand there before thee).

The Hebrew idea of God's standing before his servant is plainly spatial, and the Greek expression προ του σε is a barbarism, which perhaps suggests an abstraction.[17]

Finally, in Dt. 33: 27 there is a deliberate avoidance of calling God a " dwelling-place ":

מענה אלהי קדם

(the eternal God is a dwelling-place);

σκεπασει σε θεου αρχη

([the] power of divinity will protect thee).

The facts presented here need no further discussion. The consistency noted here in the way the LXX treats some of these expressions of motion and place in relation to God shows the presence of a definite tendency on the part of the Seventy to avoid those anthropomorphic conceptions of God which were repulsive to them.

---

[16] משכן (tent) is regularly translated by σκηνη; cf. Ex. 25: 8 (9); Lev. 17: 4; Num. 1: 50; etc.

[17] It occurs also in Lev. 18: 30 and Num. 13: 23. Rahlfs, in " Der Gebrauch der Praepositionen in der Septuaginta," by Martin Johannessohn, p. 189, n. 3, suggests that εσταναι be supplied, thus reading, " before thou takest a stand." A F have already supplied ελθειν to fill out the phrase, but this is plainly a later clarifying addition. Both A and Rahlfs' emendation bring out the idea of time for προ, which the text of B does not intend.

CHAPTER V

DIRECT AND INDIRECT SOFTENING

In this chapter we shall note several groups of examples in which the LXX, because of its tendency to spiritualize the conception of God found in the Hebrew Old Testament, definitely and purposely tones down those expressions which may seem to disparage the majesty and honor of God.

The first group includes those examples in which God is associated with some physical or tangible object and which, accordingly, are toned down in the LXX in one way or another.

Twice in the Pentateuch God is referred to as a "shield" in a metaphorical sense. In both places in the LXX the figure has been altered by expressing it with the verbal idea of "covering with a shield" ($\upsilon\pi\epsilon\rho\alpha\sigma\pi\iota\zeta\omega$), thus softening the idea considerably.

Gen. 15:1   אנכי מגן לך

(I am thy shield);

$\epsilon\gamma\omega\ \upsilon\pi\epsilon\rho\alpha\sigma\pi\iota\zeta\omega\ \sigma\sigma\upsilon$

(I am covering thee with a shield).

Dt. 33:29   מגן עזרך

(the shield of thy help);

$\upsilon\pi\epsilon\rho\alpha\sigma\pi\iota\epsilon\iota\ \sigma\ \beta\sigma\eta\theta\sigma\varsigma\ \sigma\sigma\upsilon$

(thy helper will cover [thee] with a shield).

In connection with the call of Moses to the leadership of the children of Israel, the statement is made that God will be "with his mouth" (Ex. 4:12, 15). Now in the LXX this is expressed in a more refined way, namely, that God "will open his mouth."

Ex. 4:12   ואנכי אהיה עם־פיך

(and I will be with thy mouth);

$\kappa\alpha\iota\ \epsilon\gamma\omega\ \alpha\nu\sigma\iota\xi\omega\ \tau\sigma\ \sigma\tau\sigma\mu\alpha\ \sigma\sigma\upsilon$

(and I will open thy mouth).

Ex. 4:15   ואנכי אהיה עם־פיך ועם־פיהו

(and I will be with thy mouth and his mouth);

καὶ ἐγὼ ἀνοίξω τὸ στόμα σου καὶ τὸ στόμα αὐτου

(and I will open thy mouth and his mouth).

In Ex. 17:15, the altar built by Moses is called:

י״ נסי

(Jehovah nissi).

The word, *nissi*, means "my banner," and so, literally, the name is "Jehovah is my banner." The LXX, however, cannot equate Jehovah and a banner, and accordingly renders:

Κυριος καταφυγη μου

(the Lord is my refuge).[1]

Only once is Jehovah called a sword, and that is in Dt. 33:29:

ואשר־חרב גאותך

(and who [is] the sword of thy excellency);

καὶ ἡ μαχαιρα καυχημα σου

(and the sword [shall be] thy boast).

In this way the LXX gets around the metaphor of the Hebrew.

In Ex. 33:12 and 17, there seems to be an avoidance of undue familiarity on the part of God with Moses in the LXX:

Ex. 33:12, 17   ידעתיך בשם

(I know thee by name);

οιδα σε παρα παντας

(I know thee along with [beside] all).

The undue familiarity is avoided in the LXX by substituting for the phrase "by name" the expression "along with (beside) all."[2]

---

[1] The translators connected the word with the root נום (to flee, to escape).

[2] There are three examples where the LXX has altered the verb ידע (to know) probably because of textual difficulties, and not for any theological reason.

Ex. 2:25   וידע א״

(and God knew [them]);

καὶ ἐγνωσθη αυτοις

(and he [it] was made known to them).

Greek translators read וידע אליהם.

Now follow some general examples of this softening or toning down process which come under no special heading, but which clearly show in various ways how the Seventy expressed this tendency:

Ex. 19:4   ואשא אתכם על־כנפי נשרים

(and [how] I bare you on eagles' wings);

και ανελαβον υμας ωσει επι πτερυγων αετων

(and [how] I took you up as on wings of eagles).

The metaphor is weakened into a simile in the Greek by the insertion of " as." [3]

Dt. 1:31   נשאך י״ אלהיך

(Jehovah thy God bore thee);

ετροφοφορησεν σε Κυριος ο θεος σου

(the Lord thy God sustained [brought nourishment to] thee).

The LXX has a " more decent expression than ' carry '," [4] and thus tones down the Hebrew.

Ex. 19:22   פן־יפרץ בהם י״

(lest Jehovah break forth upon them);

μη ποτε απαλλαξη απ' αυτων Κυριος

(lest the Lord depart [lit., withdraw] from them). [5]

The Greek uses a more euphemistic expression here than the Hebrew. In the following examples the translators of the LXX have avoided

Ex. 33:5   ואדעה

(that I may know);

και δειξω σοι

(and I will show you).

The Greek translators read ואדעך.

Gen. 18:19   כי ידעתיו

(for I have known him);

ηδειν οτι

(I knew that).

Greek omitted final ו, probably by haplography. Cf. Dt. 9:24.

[3] The Sam[H]. and the Vulgate agree with **M** here.
[4] Frankel, *Einfluss*, p. 216.
[5] In Ex. 19:24 the same Hebrew verb is translated by απολεση (he destroy).

the action of " setting apart " on the part of the deity by substituting the verb παραδοξαζω (to glorify). This Greek rendering was undoubtedly suggested by the Hebrew verb פלא (to be wonderful) which is pronounced in the same way as פלה (to be separated).

Ex. 8:22(18)   והפליתי ביום ההוא את־ארץ גשן

(and I will set apart in that day the land of Goshen);

καὶ παραδοξασω εν τη ημερα εκεινη την γην Γεσεμ

(and I will glorify in that day the land of Gesem).

Ex. 9:4   והפלה י'' בין מקנה ישראל ובין מקנה מצרים

(and Jehovah shall make a distinction between the cattle of Israel and the cattle of Egypt);[6]

καὶ παραδοξασω εγω εν τω καιρω εκεινω ανα μεσον των κτηνων των Αιγυπτιων καὶ ανα μεσον των κτηνων των υιων Ισραηλ

(and I will glorify in that time between the cattle of the Egyptians and between the cattle of the sons of Israel).

Ex. 11:7   יפלה י'' בין מצרים ובין ישראל

(Jehovah makes a distinction between the Egyptians and Israel);

παραδοξαζει Κυριος ανα μεσον των Αιγυπτιων και του Ισραηλ

(the Lord glorifies in the midst of the Egyptians and Israel).

In Ex. 20:23 and 30:31 we find that the Greek, by changing a pronoun in each case, considerably tones down certain statements of the Hebrew concerning God.

Ex. 20:23   לא תעשון אתי אלהי כסף

(ye shall not make with me gods of silver);

ου ποιησετε υμιν αυτοις θεους αργυρους

(ye shall not make to yourselves gods of silver).

Ex. 30:31   שמן משחת־קדש יהיה זה לי

(this shall be a holy anointing oil unto me);

Ελαιον αλιμμα χρισεως αγιον εσται τουτο υμιν

(this shall be to you a holy anointing oil).

---

[6] Sam[H]. has והפלא in Ex. 9:4, and יפלא in Ex. 11:7.

Num. 11:23   היד י״ תקצר

(Is Jehovah's hand waxed short?);

Μη χειρ Κυριου ουκ εξαρκεσει

(Will not the hand of the Lord suffice?)

The Seventy did not consider it possible that the hand of the Lord could be ineffective or powerless, since that would be inconsistent with his dignity and power. Hence the question of deficiency in the Hebrew is changed in the Greek into a question of God's sufficiency, which is a subtle but significant change in the light of our study.

In the following group certain prepositions have been changed in the LXX in order to avoid too intimate a relationship between God and that which is not divine. The translation of the examples will illustrate the point without further explanation.

Ex. 8:10(6)   אין כי״ אלהינו

(there is none like unto Jehovah our God);

ουκ εστιν αλλος πλην Κυριου

(there is not another except the Lord).

Ex. 20:3   לא יהיה־לך אלהים אחרים על־פני

(thou shalt have no other gods before me, [marg. RV, besides me]);

ουκ εσονται σοι θεοι ετεροι πλην εμου

(thou shalt have no other gods except me).

Ex. 8:22(18)   אני י״ בקרב הארץ

(I am Jehovah in the midst of the earth);

εγω ειμι Κυριος ο κυριος πασης της γης

(I am the Lord of all the earth).

Ex. 23:21   כי שמי בקרבו

(for my name is in him);

το γαρ ονομα μου εστιν επ' αυτω

(for my name is on him).

Dt. 1:42   כי אינני בקרבכם

(for I am not among you);[7]

---

[7] In the following passages בקרב is translated by εν: Num. 14:14; Dt. 23:14(15); 31:17. They have to do with the deity also, which means of course that no consistency was shown in dealing with this term in the LXX.

ου γαρ ειμι μεθ' υμων

(for I am not with you).

Ex. 20:19   אל־ידבר עמנו א״

(let not God speak with us) ;

μη λαλειτω προς ημας ο θεος

(let not God speak to us).

Ex. 24:8   אשר כרת י״ עמכם

(which Jehovah hath made with you) ;

ης διεθετο Κυριος προς υμας

(which the Lord hath made in relation to you).

Ex. 34:28   ויהי־שם עם־י״

(and he was there with Jehovah) ;

Και ην εκει Μωυσης εναντιον Κυριου

(and Moses was there before [facing] the Lord).

Lev. 25:23   כי־גרים ותושבים אתם עמדי

(for ye are strangers and sojourners with me) ;

διοτι προσηλυτοι και παροικοι υμεις εστε εναντιον μου

(for the reason that ye are strangers and sojourners before me).

Dt. 18:13   תמים תהיה עם י״ אלהיך

(thou shalt be perfect with Jehovah thy God) ;

τελειος εση εναντιον Κυριου του θεου σου

(thou shalt be perfect before the Lord thy God).

Dt. 32:39   ואין א״ עמדי

(and there is no god with me) ;[8]

και ουκ εστιν θεος πλην εμου

(and there is no god except me).

Finally we note numerous places in the LXX where terms of reproach are clearly altered to avoid disparaging the honor and dignity of God.

---

[8] But in the following passages עִם is translated by μετα: Gen. 31:5; 32:28(29); 35:3; Dt. 5:31(28). Here again no consistency is shown when this word is used with the deity.

4

In Num. 23 : 19, even though the Hebrew says that " God is not a man, that he should lie," nevertheless the LXX guards against the positive statement " that he should lie " by throwing it into the passive voice:

ויכזב

(that he should lie) ;

διαρτηθηναι

(to be deceived).[9]

Num. 16 : 22   ועל כל־העדה תקצף

(and wilt thou be wroth with all the congregation?) ;

επι πασαν την συναγωγην οργη Κυριου

(on all the gathering [will there be] wrath of the Lord?).

The direct and personal statement concerning the deity "wilt thou be wroth" has been toned down considerably in the LXX by the use of the abstract noun "wrath" modified by the genitive phrase " of the Lord."

In Dt. 23 : 14(15) the passive voice is employed in the LXX in order to have an expression theologically more refined:

ולא יראה בך ערות דבר

(and he will not see in thee a nakedness of a thing, i. e., an indecency) ;

και ουκ οφθησεται εν σοι ασχημοσυνη πραγματος

(and there will not be seen in thee an indecency of a thing).

Even in those cases where God is not the subject, but the object of some part of the reproachful expression, the LXX alters the conception in its translation, lest the honor of God be damaged.

In Gen. 18 : 25 the expression חללה לך is found twice, meaning " far be it from thee," i. e., from God, to do such and such a thing. Now the form, חללה from the root חלל (to profane, to pollute), is taken as a substantive, with the ה terminative, and used as an exclamation, literally, " ad profanum." The Greek evidently felt the presence of negation in this word, and by avoiding the literal rendering, gives the facile translation, μηδαμως συ ποιησεις in v. 25a (thou shalt not do [it] at all), and μηδαμως in v. 25b (not at all).

---

[9] ויכזב may have been read as a Pual. In the light of two other anti-anthropomorphisms and anti-anthropopathies in this verse, see pp 9, 18, the change was probably deliberate.

Ex. 22:28(27)   א״ לא תקלל

(thou shalt not revile God [marg. RV, the judges]);

Θεους ου κακολογησεις

(gods thou shalt not speak ill of).

The Greek very plainly cannot tolerate the idea of reviling the true and living God, and so the plural form of the noun is used.[10]

In Lev. 24:10-16 the story is told of the man who blasphemed " the Name " and cursed. The verses which are affected in the LXX are the following:

Lev. 24:11

ויקב בן־האשה הישראלית את־השם ויקלל

(and the son of the Israelitish woman blasphemed the Name and cursed);

και επονομασας ο υιος της γυναικος της Ισραηλειτιδος το ονομα κατηρασατο

(and the son of the Israelitish woman, having pronounced the Name, cursed).

Lev. 24:15[11]

Lev. 24:16a   ונקב שם־י״

(he that blasphemeth the name of Jehovah);

ονομαζων δε το ονομα Κυριου

(and addressing by name the name of the Lord).

Lev. 24:16b   בנקבו־שם

(when he blasphemeth the name);

εν τω ονομασαι αυτον το ονομα Κυριου

(when he addresses by name the name of the Lord).

As we study these verses, several things are quite evident. First, the expressions ויקב את־השם (v. 11) and בנקבו־שם (v. 16b) are parallels of נקב שם־י״ (v. 16a). There is little reason to hold that in these three passages שם was introduced as a surrogate for Jehovah

---

[10] See Gordon, " אלהים in its Reputed Meaning of ' Rulers, Judges '," *JBL*, LIV, p. 143. It should be noted that the form אלהים is plural in Hebrew, and so there is grammatical justification for the rendering Θεους.

[11] See p. 25.

by later hands.[12]   The half-breed, according to the narrative, was guilty of blaspheming the name of the Lord, not the Lord, and so was condemned to death.   Secondly, there should be noted the translation of נקב (to calumniate, to curse) in v. 11 [13] and v. 16 by ονομαζω (also επονομαζω).   Now this translation of the Greek may be justified from the Hebrew verb root, which means " to bore, to pierce, to mark, to distinguish," and ultimately, by semantic development, " to indicate by name."   But in v. 11, this verb is used as a synonym of קלל which in the Piel can only mean "to curse " from the idea of " making light of, making contemptible."   The LXX, however, has taken the much less reproachful meaning, and has used it throughout these verses for the translation of נקב in order not to express the possibility of such a blasphemy.   And thirdly, it is wrong to derive the belief in the unutterableness of Jehovah's name from this passage as it is translated in the LXX.   The mere naming of Jehovah's name is not worthy of death, but whoever names the name of the Lord in a curse will die.[14]

Another and final example of avoiding a reproachful term in connection with God is found in Num. 15 : 30 :

את־ל״ הוא מגדף

(the same blasphemeth Jehovah) ;

τον θεον ουτος παροξυνει

(this one irritates [provokes] God).

Having dealt with those expressions which the Seventy toned down because either God was described in undignified terms, or his actions were considered unseemly, we now turn to another group of passages which have been modified by softening in the LXX.   In these instances

---

[12] It has been suggested that שם is unheard of in Biblical Hebrew in this sense, and must have been introduced by later hands because of the awe that came to be attached to the name of Jehovah.   Cf. Dalman, *Der Gottesname Adonaj*, p. 45; Geiger, *Urschrift*, p. 274; Strack, *Leviticus*, p. 357, in *Kommentar*.

[13] The form ויקב in v. 11 is probably from נקב (so König and G-B), although it might come from קבב (so B-D-B).   As to the two roots נקב and קבב (to curse) G-B suggests either that they are related etymologically, or that קבב was purposely changed into נקב, which König rejects.   The verb נקב comes to mean " curse " from the idea of perforating or punching through something and so injuring or harming it.

[14] Dalman, *op. cit.*, pp. 44, 45.

God may be the object, toward whom there is directed some action, physical or mental, or the name of God may stand in a genitive relation to some noun. Here the original sense was altered to correspond with the more spiritual conception of God which is found in the LXX. It is these cases which may be called examples of "indirect softening."

In Gen. 50:19, Joseph, comforting his brethren, makes the statement:

.   אל־תיראו כי התחת א״ אני

(fear not: for am I in the place of God?)

The Greek tones this down considerably when it says:

Μη φοβεισθε, του γαρ θεου εγω ειμι

(fear not, for I am God's).

Even the thought that one could be in the place of God is avoided in the Greek.

Ex. 19:21   פן־יהרסו אל־י״

(lest they break through to Jehovah);

μη ποτε εγγισωσιν προς τον θεον

(lest perchance they draw near to God).

The Greek verb εγγισωσιν is a softening of the Hebrew "break through."

The example of this anti-anthropomorphic tendency in the LXX, which is cited most frequently as an illustration by writers who mention this phenomenon in the Greek Old Testament, is the one found in Ex. 24:10 and 11. In this case it is actually said that certain men saw God. Yet in this same book, Ex. 33:20, the Lord specifically said to Moses: "Thou canst not see my face; for man shall not see me and live." The LXX naturally finds it necessary to remove such a crass anthropomorphism, and so in the Greek, the men do not see God, but "the place where God stood":

Ex. 24:10   ויראו את אלהי ישראל

(and they saw the God of Israel);

και ειδον τον τοπον ου ιστηκει ο θεος του Ισραηλ

(and they saw the place where the God of Israel stood).

Ex. 24:11   ויחזו את־הא״

(and they beheld God);

κατ ωφθησαν εν τω τοπω του θεου

(and they appeared in the place of God).[15]

In Ex. 13:12 we read "that thou shalt set apart unto Jehovah all that openeth the womb, and every firstling which thou hast that cometh of a beast; the males shall be Jehovah's." The Greek avoids the idea of Jehovah's possessing something, as expressed in the last clause, in the following way:

הזכרים לי״

(the males [shall be] Jehovah's);

τα αρσενικα αγιασεις τω κυριω

(the males thou shalt consecrate to the Lord).

At the divine manifestation described in Lev. 9:24, the people "shouted" (וירנו) and fell on their faces. The Greek does not translate the verb "shout," but in its place uses εξεστη (they were astonished); the reason might have been that "shouting" was not considered proper on such a hallowed occasion.[16]

Then there is the expression לחם א״ (the bread of God), used in Leviticus and Numbers as a sacrificial term, which, because of its obviously objectionable meaning to the Seventy, was taken over into the LXX as (τα) δωρα του θεου (the gifts of God).

Lev. 21:6   לחם אלהיהם

(the bread [food] of their God);

δωρα του θεου αυτων

(gifts of their God).[17]

---

[15] Sam^H., ויאחזו (and they took hold of). There is an instance in Ex. 19:21 where the Greek translates לראות by κατανοησαι (to observe, to perceive); but this is not a softening for two reasons: first, because the two words mean very nearly the same thing, and secondly, because this same word is found in the Greek as a translation of ראה in Gen. 42:9; Ex. 2:11; Num. 32:8, 9, where God is neither the subject nor the object of the verb.

[16] So Frankel, *op. cit.*, p. 130.

[17] So also in Lev. 21:8, 17, 21, 22; 22:25; Num. 28:24. In Lev. 3:11 and 16, the phrase לחם אשה (food of the offering made by fire) is rendered simply by καρπωμα (fruit), which is the usual translation of אשה alone in the LXX. Thus לחם has been omitted here, unless it may have been included in the term καρπωμα.

The Hebrew expression לחם הפנים (the bread of the face, or, of the presence), translated "showbread" and in the margin of the Revised Version, "Presence-bread," has been rendered in various ways in the LXX:

Num. 28: 2   לחמי

(my bread [food]);

δοματα μου

(my gifts).

In Lev. 17: 6, the altar, upon which the priest sprinkles the blood,
is called "the altar of Jehovah":

על־מזבח י״

(upon the altar of Jehovah).

But the Greek refuses to make Jehovah the possessor of an altar and
uses a circumlocution:

επι το θυσιαστηριον κυκλω απεναντι Κυριου

(upon the altar round about before the Lord).

In Num. 11: 20 the statement is made that Jehovah's people had
"rejected" him; the verb here used is מאס (to reject, to despise).
This idea has been softened in the Greek by translating the word by
απειθεω (to disobey).

יען כי־מאסתם את־י״

(because that ye rejected Jehovah);

οτι ηπειθησατε Κυριω

(because ye disobeyed the Lord).[18]

Ex. 25: 29 (30)	αρτους ενωπιους (presence loaves).
Ex. 39: 18 (36)	τους αρτους τους προκειμενους (the loaves which lie before).
Ex. 40: 21 (23)	αρτους της προθεσεως (loaves of the setting forth).

It is clear that the translators did not take פנים as a surrogate for God,
as it is in Ex. 33: 14, 15 and Dt. 4: 37, but rather in the same sense as it
has in the prepositional phrase לפני, "to the face of," "before," "in the
presence of," the idea being that the bread was lying on the table in the
presence of, or before, Jehovah.

[18] This expression is not modified in the Greek of Num. 14: 31, where it
speaks of "rejecting" the land; but in Lev. 26: 15, where it speaks of
"rejecting" God's statutes, the Greek again has απειθεω. The verb απωθεω
(to thrust off, to reject), which would have probably been the literal translation of מאס may have suggested the verb απειθεω, because of their close
similarity. At any rate, through απειθεω we can see probably what the literal
translation should have been: an expression which was deliberately avoided.

The Greek makes a differentiation in Num. 21: 5 between speaking "against God and against Moses," as the Hebrew has it. The passage is as follows:

וידבר העם באלהים ובמשה

(and the people spoke against God and against Moses) ;

και κατελαλει ο λαος προς τον θεον και κατα Μωυση

(and the people spoke to God and against Moses).

The Seventy obviously intended to make a fine distinction here by using two different prepositions. In Num. 21: 7, however, where the same phrase occurs, the same preposition κατα is used in both places, perhaps purposely to retain the original idea in close proximity to v. 5, where the expression had been modified.

In Num. 24: 4 we read:

אשר מחזה שדי יחזה נפל וגלוי עינים

(Who seeth the vision of the Almighty, fallen down, yet having his eyes open) ;

οστις ορασιν θεου ειδεν, εν υπνω, αποκεκαλυμμενοι οι οφθαλμοι αυτου

(Who saw a vision of God in sleep, his eyes open).[19]

The Hebrew means of course that Balaam had fallen because he was overcome by the Spirit of God. The Greek omits this, but substitutes the idea of sleeping during which the vision appeared, and thus subtly avoids the idea of actually beholding the vision in a conscious moment.

In Dt. 9: 18, 25 Moses speaks of flinging himself down before Jehovah in the scene where he intercedes for the children of Israel after they had made the golden calf:

ואתנפל לפני י״

(and I flung myself down before Jehovah).

The LXX renders this expression as follows:

και εδεηθην εναντιον Κυριου

(and I begged before the Lord).

Here the Greek does away with the idea that one can fall down physically before the deity. The Greek verb used was undoubtedly suggested by the Hebrew verb פלל (hithpael, to intercede, to pray) because of its similarity in sound to נפל. Thus, the sense of imploring, which is implied in the Hebrew, is brought out in the Greek by this deliberate device.

---

[19] Identical expression in Num. 24: 16.

CHAPTER VI

GRAMMATICAL CHANGES

In this chapter we shall deal with three main groups of grammatical
changes which by their presence in the Greek text show how the
Seventy tried to remove the idea that God participates in the affairs
of this world. In this way they tried to attain a more spiritual conception of the deity.

The first group is that in which the Hebrew active verb of which
God is the subject, is rendered by a passive in the Greek; the second
group, of which there are fewer examples, is composed of those instances where the active verb of the Hebrew, again with God as subject,
is rendered by an impersonal construction; and the last group consists of a number of cases where the person of the verb is changed so
that God is no longer the subject of the sentence.

Since the examples will be clear without further explanation, they
will be cited according to the categories given above. Textual matters
will be discussed in the footnotes.

First group, active voice in Hebrew, passive in Greek:

Gen. 15:6   ויחשבה לו צדקה

  (and he reckoned it to him as righteousness);

  καɩ ελογισθη αυτω εɩς δικαιοσυνην

(and it was reckoned to him for righteousness).[1]

Ex. 9:16   ואולם בעבור זאת העמדתיך

(but in very deed for this cause have I made thee to stand);

  καɩ ενεκεν τουτου διετηρηθης

(and on this account you were watched closely).

Ex. 32:29   ולתת עליכם היום ברכה

(that he may bestow upon you this day a blessing);

  δοθηναι εφ' υμας ευλογιαν

(that a blessing may be given you).

---

[1] In Ps. 105(106):31 the Hebrew has the passive voice in this same expression, and the Greek translated it exactly as in this passage.

Ex. 36 : 1   אשר נתן י׳ חכמה ותבונה בהמה

(in whom Jehovah hath put wisdom and understanding) ;

ω εδοθη σοφια και επιστημη εν αυτοις

(to whom wisdom and understanding were given).

Lev. 10 : 6   את־השרפה אשר שרף י׳

(the burning which Jehovah kindled) ;

τον ενπυρισμον ον ενεπυρισθησαν υπο Κυριου

(the burning in respect to which they were enkindled by the Lord).

Lev. 23 : 30   והאבדתי את־הנפש ההוא

(and that soul will I destroy) ;

απολειται η ψυχη εκεινη

(that soul shall perish).

Num. 12 : 5   ויקרא אהרן ומרים

(and he [Jehovah] called Aaron and Miriam) ;

και εκληθησαν Ααρων και Μαριαμ

(and Aaron and Miriam were called).

Dt. 2 : 30   למען תתו בידך

(that he [Jehovah] might deliver him into thy hand) ;

ινα παραδοθη εις τας χειρας σου

(that he might be delivered into thy hands).

Dt. 4 : 36   השמיעך את־קלו

(he [Jehovah] made thee to hear his voice) ;

ακουστη εγενετο η φωνη αυτου

(his voice became audible).[2]

---

[2] In Ex. 40 : 28, 29 (34, 35), even the active verb " fill," of which the subject
is the glory of the Lord, is thrown into the passive voice in Greek :

וכבוד י׳ מלא את־המשכן

(and the glory of the Lord filled the tabernacle) ;

και δοξης Κυριου επλησθη η σκηνη

(and the tabernacle was filled with the glory of the Lord).

It should be noted that this change from the active voice of the verb in Hebrew
to the passive voice in the Greek is not limited to verbs whose actions are
connected with God. Cf. Dt. 17 : 10. There are cases even of Hebrew passive

The second group consists of a few instances of impersonal constructions in the Greek, which, in the Hebrew, have God as the subject:

Ex. 5:3   פן־יפגענו בדבר או בחרב

(lest he fall upon us with pestilence, or with the sword);

μη ποτε συναντηση ημιν θανατος η φονος

(lest perchance death or slaughter befall [meet with] us).

Ex. 10:1   למען שתי אתתי אלה

(that I may show these my signs);

ινα εξης επελθη τα σημεια ταυτα επ' αυτους

(in order that one after the other these signs may come upon them).

Lev. 26:33   והריקתי אחריכם חרב

(and I will draw out a sword after you);

και εξαναλωσει υμας επιπορευομενη η μαχαιρα

(and the sword, coming upon [you], shall utterly destroy you).

Third group: those cases where the person of the verb has been changed, obviously to avoid having God the subject of the sentence.

Ex. 1:21   ויעש להם בתים

(and he [God] made them households);

εποιησαν εαυταις οικιας

(and they made houses for themselves).

Ex. 16:32   אשר האכלתי אתכם

(wherewith I fed you);

ον εφαγετε υμεις

(which you ate).

Ex. 23:7   כי לא־אצדיק רשע

(for I will not justify the wicked);

verbs being rendered by the active voice in Greek. Cf. Gen. 12:15; 25:10; Ex. 27:7; Num. 36:2. Could it be possible that the translators of the LXX had a different Hebrew text before them from our Masoretic text? At any rate it is questionable whether the examples of the change from the active to the passive in the text above are due entirely to an anti-anthropomorhic tendency. Other factors which are not apparent now may have been involved.

και ου δικαιωσεις τον ασεβη ενεκεν δωρων

(nor shalt thou justify the wicked man on account of gifts).[3]

Ex. 34:9   ונחלתנו

(and take us for thine inheritance);

και εσομεθα σοι

(and we shall be to thee).

Dt. 2:22

כאשר עשה לבני עשו . . . אשר השמיד את־החרי

(as he did for the children of Esau when he destroyed the Horites);

ωσπερ εποιησαν τοις υιοις Ησαν . . . ον τροπον εξετριψαν τον Χορραιον

(as they did to the sons of Esau in the manner that they destroyed the Horites).[4]

Dt. 4:10   ואשמעם את־דברי

(and I will make them hear my words);

και ακουσατωσαν τα ρηματα μου

(and let them hear my words).

Dt. 6:24   לחיתנו

(that he might preserve us alive);

ινα ζωμεν

(that we may live).

Dt. 32:13   וינקהו דבש מסלע

(and he made him to suck honey from the rock);

εθηλασαν μελι εκ πετρας

(they sucked honey from the rock).

[3] In this verse there appears to be a leveling of the subject to the same person as that which is found in the preceding and following verses. That is, the pronoun "thou" precedes and follows this verse in the Hebrew, and the pronoun "I," referring to God, seems to break the continuity of thought. Therefore, "I" is rejected in the Greek and "thou" is substituted to keep the verse in line with the context. Probably, then, to make the passage read intelligibly, the phrase "on account of gifts" was added from the following verse.

Sam[H]., הצדיק. Proposed emendation: ולא תצדיק, according to the Greek: Quell, in Kittel's *Biblia Hebraica*.

[4] εποιησαν B] εποιησε A F M, but no difference between B and A in εξετριψαν.

Dt. 34:6   וַיִּקְבֹּר אֹתוֹ

(and he [Jehovah] buried him [Moses]);

και εθαψαν αυτον

(and they buried him).[5]

---

[5] The translation with Jehovah as subject is found in all the versions except the LXX. The Hebrew form does permit of an impersonal construction, "one buried him," and so the LXX, "they buried him," or "he was buried" (JV and marg. RV); but in view of 6b "but no man knoweth of his sepulchre," Jehovah was doubtless meant to be the subject. So Driver, *Deuteronomy* (*ICC*), p. 423; Oettli, *Deuteronomium*, p. 120, in Strack and Zochler, *Kommentar*; Bertholet, *Deuteronomium*, p. 113, in *Kurzer Hand-Kommentar*. The LXX, by making the verb plural, avoids all doubt as to whether the form was impersonal or had Jehovah as subject.

Again there are numerous cases where this change of the person of the verb in the LXX has nothing to do with the deity; cf. Ex. 19:16; 25:2; Dt. 6:2.

CHAPTER VII

Intermediary Elements

Another method used by the Seventy to represent a more spiritual
conception of God was to interpose between God and his interests in
this world an intermediary element which would thereby set him apart
and aloof from mundane affairs. It is important to note, however,
that we find no such highly developed scheme of intermediaries in
the LXX, as we do in the Targums, with their Shekinah (שכינתא),
Word (מימרא, מאמרא) and Glory (יקרא), or in Philo with his Logos
and intermediary powers. The medial elements in the LXX for the
most part are merely expressed by grammatical circumlocutions which
can easily be classified into two main groups.

In the first group, the simple genitive relationship, like " God's
house," is rendered in the Greek by the phrase " the house from
(παρα) God," or " the house which is from God." By the interposition
of this preposition the Greek produces a distinct gap between God and
the object possessed which is not present in the simple genitive (construct) relationship of the Hebrew. The examples are as follows:

Gen. 23 : 6 נשיא א״

(a prince of God);

βασιλευς παρα θεου

(a king from God);

Ex. 4 : 20 את־מטה הא״

(the rod of God);

την ραβδον την παρα του θεου

(the rod from God).

Ex. 14 : 13 את־ישועת י״

(the salvation of Jehovah);

την σωτηριαν την παρα του θεου

(the salvation from God).

Lev. 10 : 7 שמן משחת י״

(the anointing oil of Jehovah);

το . . . ελαιον της χρισεως το παρα Κυριου

(the oil of the anointing from the Lord).

Num. 11 : 1, 3
אש י״

(the fire of Jehovah) ;

πυρ παρα Κυριου

(a fire from the Lord).

Num. 24 : 16
דעת עליון

(the knowledge of the Most High) ;

επιστημην παρα Υψιστου

(knowledge from the Most High).

Num. 31 : 3
נקמת־י״

(the vengeance of Jehovah) ;

εκδικησιν παρα του κυριου

(vengeance from the Lord).

Dt. 33 : 23
ברכת י״

(the blessing of Jehovah) ;

ευλογιαν παρα Κυριου

(a blessing from the Lord).

The second group consists of those cases in which the Greek expression τα προς τον θεον (κυριον) has been substituted for the simple אלהים or יהוה. It is quite obvious that the neuter plural article with the preposition has been interposed in the Greek to serve as a verbal buffer between God and his activities in this world. The examples are as follows:

Ex. 4 : 16
ואתה תהיה־לו לא״

(and thou shalt be to him for God) ;

συ δε αυτω εση τα προς τον θεον

(but thou shalt be to him those things relating to God).

Ex. 18 : 19
היה אתה לעם מול הא״

(be thou for the people before God) ;

γινου συ τω λαω τα προς τον θεον

(be thou to the people the things relating to God).

Dt. 1:36   יען אשר מלא אחרי י״

(because that he hath wholly followed after Jehovah);

δια το προσκεισθαι αυτον τα προς Κυριον

(because he is devoted to the things relating to the Lord).

Dt. 9:7, 24   ממרים הייתם עם־י״

(ye have been rebellious against Jehovah);

απειθουντες διετελειτε τα προς Κυριον

(you have continued disobeying the things relating to the Lord).

Dt. 31:27   ממרים היתם עם־י״

(you have been rebellious against Jehovah);

παραπικραινοντες ητε τα προς τον θεον

(you were provoking [lit., embittering] the things relating to God).[1]

In addition to these two groups are several examples which fall under no special classification, but which very clearly illustrate this intermediating principle.

In Ex. 4:24 we read that Jehovah met Moses. This expression of God's meeting with some one has been quite consistently avoided in the LXX, as has been noted above.[2] Here, however, the verb is translated literally in the Greek, but a personal intermediary is introduced.

ויפגשהו י״

(and Jehovah met him);

συνηντησεν αυτω αγγελος Κυριου

(an angel of the Lord met him).

Ex. 18:15   לדרש א״

(to inquire of God);

εκζητησαι κρισιν παρα του θεου

(to seek judgment from God).

---

[1] It must be noted that in neither of these cases—παρα c. gen. and τα προς c. acc.—are the translators making use of a set pattern of translation. In the Pentateuch there are no examples of παρα c. gen. used as a substitute for the genitive except those examples quoted in the text. τα προς c. acc. does not occur in Genesis although προς c. acc. is found some 300 times in that book. το προς is found for לעת in Gen. 8:11 and 24:11. Cf. Thackeray, *Grammar*, p. 40.

[2] See above, pp. 30-32.

The LXX derives this rendering from the context of the passage which narrates the incident of Jethro's advice in regard to the appointment of judges to relieve Moses. It is a deliberate interposition of a direct object and it makes good sense.

Ex. 19:3   ומשה עלה אל־הא״

(and Moses went up to God);

καὶ Μωυσης ανεβη εις το ορος του θεου

(and Moses went up to the mountain of God).

The reason for inserting "mountain" in the LXX is obvious, since the translators felt that Moses could not go up to God. Although the Seventy found the word in the same verse just a few words beyond, the addition in the LXX beyond a doubt was made with a definite purpose in view, and was not a scribal error.

Ex. 21:6   והגישו אדניו אל־הא״

(then his master shall bring him to God, [marg. RV, the judges]);

προσαξει αυτον ο κυριος αυτου προς το κριτηριον του θεου

(his lord shall bring him to the tribunal of God).

Instead of rendering אלהים by a plural, as is done in a somewhat similar case in Ex. 22:28(27),[3] the Greek here keeps the singular του θεου, but introduces το κριτηριον between אל and אלהים. Thus the shocking implications of the idea of bringing some one to God are avoided.[4]

---

[3] See above, p. 43.

[4] Onkelos reads דיניא (judges); V diis (gods).

As further examples of this tendency of inserting intermediaries in the Greek, cf. Lev. 6:2 and Dt. 32:51 (pp. 60, 61).

5

CHAPTER VIII

MISCELLANEOUS MATTERS

Under this title there will be treated two points which do not bear
directly on the subject under consideration, but which are so closely
connected with it that they should be noted.

The first to be noted is a different psychological attitude on the
part of the translators of the LXX. It is a commonplace to say that
in the Old Testament the Hebrew expresses himself in exceedingly
concrete and picturesque language, and that his thinking is often
highly colored with emotion. One of the best and most common
examples of this is found in the use of the word לב (heart). The
Hebrew loves with his heart and thinks with his heart (Ex. 36:1);
he eats in order to strengthen his heart (Gen. 18:5). It is in these
instances that the LXX translation shows the influence of the Greek
milieu in which it was produced. The important thing for the Greek
was the mind, and not the heart, as with the Hebrew. Therefore in
these expressions the LXX has shifted the emphasis from the heart
to the mind. For example:

Gen. 6:6   ויתעצב אל־לבו

(and it grieved him at his heart);

$$\kappa\alpha\iota\ \delta\iota\epsilon\nu o\eta\theta\eta$$

(and he reflected [considered well]).

Gen. 8:21   ויאמר י׳׳ אל־לבו

(and the Lord said to himself [lit., to his heart]);

$$\kappa\alpha\iota\ \epsilon\iota\pi\epsilon\nu\ \mathrm{K}\upsilon\rho\iota os\ o\ \theta\epsilon os\ \delta\iota\alpha\nu o\eta\theta\epsilon\iota s$$

(and the Lord God said, thinking it over).

According to H-R, the noun $\delta\iota\alpha\nu o\iota\alpha$ (mind) is used as the translation of לב or לבב (heart) twenty-six times in the Pentateuch. One
illustration of this type suffices:

Gen. 24:45   טרם אכלה לדבר אל־לבי

(before I had done speaking to myself [lit., to my heart]);

$$\pi\rho o\ \tau o\upsilon\ \sigma\upsilon\nu\tau\epsilon\lambda\epsilon\sigma\alpha\iota\ \mu\epsilon\ \lambda\alpha\lambda o\upsilon\nu\tau\alpha\ \epsilon\nu\ \tau\eta\ \delta\iota\alpha\nu o\iota\alpha\ \mu o\upsilon$$

(before I had finished speaking in my mind).

The second point to be considered in this chapter is the way in which the LXX deals with the problem of sin. The tendency to spiritualize the conception of God in the LXX, in opposition to the anthropomorphic idea of God in the Hebrew Old Testament, naturally affected the conception of sin. The result of this anti-anthropomorphic tendency of the Greek translation of the Old Testament has been to remove God from man and the affairs of this world. Thus, man does not sin "against" God, but "before" him; he does not "deal treacherously" with God, but merely "overlooks" or "forgets" God or the laws of God.

An example of this is found in the translation of the phrase חטא ל (to sin against). When one sins against God, the prepositions ενωπιον, εναντιον, or εναντι are used, meaning "before," "in the presence of." When the idea of sinning against man is expressed the prepositions εις or προς are used. One example of each expression follows:

Gen. 39 : 9   וחטאתי לא"

(and I will sin against God);

και αμαρτησομαι εναντιον του θεου

(and I will sin before God).[1]

Gen. 20 : 9   ומה־חטאתי לך

` (and how have I sinned against thee);

μη τι ημαρτομεν εις σε

(have we sinned against thee in any way).[2]

In Ex. 10:16, both expressions are found in the same verse, and the LXX makes a clear distinction between sinning against God and against man:

חטאתי לי" אלהיכם ולכם

(I have sinned against Jehovah your God, and against you);

Ημαρτηκα εναντιον Κυριου του θεου υμων και εις υμας

(I have sinned before the Lord your God and against you).

---

[1] So also Gen. 13: 13; Ex. 32: 33; Num. 32: 23; Dt. 1: 41, 9: 16, 20: 18. Cf. Lev. 4: 2,   נפש כי־תחטא

(if anyone shall sin);

Ψυχη εαν αμαρτη εναντι Κυριου

(if anyone shall sin before the Lord),

where the Greek adds the final phrase.

[2] So also Gen. 43: 9, 44: 32.

Two more examples in this connection must be mentioned. They
are apparently exceptions to the ones above.

Gen. 20: 6   ואחשך גם־אנכי אותך מחטו־לי

    (and I also withheld thee from sinning against me) ;

    και εφεισαμην εγω σου του μη αμαρτειν σε εις εμε

    (and I saved thee from sinning against me).

Ex. 23: 33   פן־יחטיאו אתך לי

    (lest they make thee sin against me) ;

    ινα μη αμαρτειν σε ποιησωσιν προς με

    (lest they make thee to sin against me).

In considering these passages, however, we note that God himself is
the speaker. Accordingly, since he himself says, " sin against me,"
the expression may be carried over into the Greek literally without
contradicting any of the statements made above.[3]

Another example of the same type is the way in which the Seventy
translate the Hebrew verb מעל. The meaning of this verb is " to act
unfaithfully, treacherously " against some one. When such an action
is directed against God, the LXX tones down the phrase in one way
or another to avoid the idea that God may be treacherously dealt with.
The examples are as follows :

Lev. 6: 2 (5: 21)   ומעלה מעל בי״

    (and acts treacherously against Jehovah) ;

    και παριδων παριδη τας εντολας Κυριου

    (and utterly disregards the laws of the Lord).

Lev. 26: 40   במעלם אשר מעלו־בי

    (in their treacherous act which they acted against me) ;

    οτι παρεβησαν και υπερειδον με

    (because they transgressed and overlooked me).

---

[3] Compare also Num. 27: 3:

    הנועדים על־י״

    (who gathered themselves together against Jehovah);

    της επισυστασης εναντι Κυριου

    (of the riotous meeting before the Lord).

But in Num. 14: 35 and 16: 11 the preposition על is translated literally in
the Greek in the same expression by επι and προς respectively.

Num. 5:6   למעל מעל בי״

(in order to act treacherously against Jehovah);

παριδων παριδη

(utterly disregards).

Num. 31:16   למסר־מעל בי״

(to commit [offer] a treacherous act against Jehovah);

υπεριδειν το ρημα Κυριου

(to overlook the word of the Lord).

Dt. 32:51   על אשר מעלתם בי

(because you acted treacherously against me);

οτι ηπειθησατε τω ρηματι μου

(because you disobeyed my word).

CONCLUSION

An anti-anthropomorphic tendency has long been observed in the Greek Old Testament; in this investigation its extent in the Pentateuch has been ascertained, the examples have been classified, and certain conclusions have been drawn. Actual anthropomorphisms and anthropopathies are taken over into the Greek with comparatively few cases of alteration; on the other hand, there are some anthropomorphic expressions and metaphors which are quite consistently avoided in the Greek.

It has been noted in this study that in the case of expressions where the LXX quite consistently renders the Hebrew anthropomorphism literally, one exception is usually present where a reverential paraphrase or surrogate is employed.[1] Furthermore, where the LXX quite consistently avoids the anthropomorphism of the Hebrew, there is usually found one example where the literal rendering is retained in the Greek.[2] The Seventy accordingly seem to have followed a definite system in these cases.

It has been observed, however, that, for the most part, the LXX reveals no consistent method of avoiding the anthropomorphisms of the Hebrew. Genesis and Leviticus, for instance, are singularly free from anti-anthropomorphisms in the Greek, whereas Exodus has the most examples of any book in the Pentateuch. Comparatively speaking, the poetical passages contain more examples of this anti-anthropomorphic tendency than the prose sections. There are even some cases where the LXX is more anthropomorphic than the Hebrew.[3]

The tendency to spiritualize the conception of God in the LXX by avoiding anthropomorphic expressions was active; it was not strong enough, however, to make itself felt consistently, except in a comparatively few instances. In this connection it must be borne in mind that the Seventy did not undertake to rewrite the Pentateuch. They were translators, but in various passages their theology is brought out in this version.

---

[1] See pp. 14(יד); 19(קָצַף) and (קֶצֶף).

[2] See pp. 13(אֹזֶן); 28(פסח); 30(יעד); 32(קרה); 34(שכן).

[3] Ex. 15: 5   תהמת יכסימו
(the deeps cover them);

62

Finally, consideration must be given to the possible origin of this anti-anthropomorphic tendency. As has already been stated,[4] there are two schools of thought on this matter. A few scholars like Frankel, Freudenthal and Wendland,[5] hold that this tendency is inherent in Judaism itself, whereas a larger number of scholars[6] maintain that it is due to Greek influence. From this study certain observations point definitely to the latter opinion. The emphasis the LXX puts upon the mind (διανοια) in comparison with the Hebrew's emphasis upon the heart (לב)[7] is not a change wrought by Jewish theologians, but it is a distinct Grecism. In Alexandria, the home of the LXX, Greek was a necessity in the daily life of the Jewish residents. Each succeeding generation became more conversant with Greek and gradually lost its familiarity with Hebrew and Aramaic. The current Greek psychology and modes of thought naturally would affect a translation

ποντω εκαλυψεν αυτους
(with the sea he covered them).

Ex. 33: 13   הודעני נא את־דרכך
(show me, I pray thee, thy way);

εμφανισον μοι σεαυτον
(manifest thyself to me).

Ex. 33: 18   הראני נא את־כבדך
(show me, I pray thee, thy glory);

εμφανισον μοι σεαυτον
(manifest thyself to me).

Ex. 34: 34   אתאשר יצוה
(that which he was commanded);

οσα ενετειλατο αυτω Κυριος
(as many things as the Lord commanded him).

Lev. 8: 35   כי־כן צויתי
(for thus I am commanded);

ουτως γαρ ενετειλατο μοι Κυριος ο θεος
(for so the Lord God commanded me).

Dt. 33: 21   צדקת י״ עשה
(he performed the righteousness of Jehovah);

δικαιοσυνην Κυριος εποιησεν
(the Lord performed righteousness).

[4] See pp. 3, 4.
[5] See p. 4; also Wendland, *Kultur*, p. 203.
[6] See pp. 3, 4; also Bois, *Origines*, p. 131, Drummond, *Philo*, pp. 156-66.
[7] See p. 58.

made for a Jewish community almost a hundred years after its founding in Alexandria.

It is highly improbable that we can go so far as Dähne when he says that the translators had already become familiar with the principles of Philonic philosophy,[8] and his attempt to find a full-fledged Alexandrian philosophical system is not convincing.

A true perspective of the problem is attained if we consider the LXX in its proper chronological place and note the development of this anti-anthropomorphic tendency from the Hebrew, through the LXX, to its climax in Philo. This is illustrated by an example which has been discussed above.[9] The personal character of God is reflected in Ex. 3:14, where he says that אהיה (I am) will send Moses to deliver Israel. The LXX, however, has somewhat depersonalized this proper name (an imperfect tense, 1st person singular) by rendering it as a participle, although retaining the masculine gender ὁ ὤν. It is not yet a pure abstraction. But when we come to Philo, we find that besides the term ὁ ὤν which is applied to God, he also uses the neuter article with the present participle, τὸ ὄν, which is a pure abstraction. Thus the change from אהיה to ὁ ὤν to τὸ ὄν is a graphic illustration of the way in which Greek speculation and philosophy influenced Judaism. This was, for the most part, a purely philosophical procedure, culminating in Philo, whose main purpose was to reconcile Judaism with Greek thought.

The anti-anthropomorphic tendency which began in the Old Testament and was further developed in Judaism has sometimes been confused with that which is found in the LXX and in Philo. They are, however, two quite different things. The former was due, not to philosophical adjustments, like the latter, but rather to theological developments amongst the Jews themselves. When the people were no longer permitted to pronounce the divine name (יהוה), it became necessary to find surrogates. This inevitably led to the introduction of intermediaries who stood between God and this world, and who assumed many of the duties of the transcendent deity.[10] But God does not become an abstract conception in the Targums, for instance, as he does in Philo. The view of Weber[11] and his followers, who maintain that the Rabbis taught an abstract monotheism, or a trans-

---

[8] Dähne, *op. cit.*, p. 3.

[9] See p. 22.

[10] See p. 54.   [11] Weber, *System, passim.*

cendent idea of God as the Absolute, has been shown to be false by a number of Jewish and Christian scholars.[12] The transcendent God of rabbinic theology is at the same time a personal God; the Absolute of Philo is a pure abstraction.

There appear to be then two streams of anti-anthropomorphic development in Jewish history. One goes its own way through the Old Testament into the rabbinical period, confined to the Hebrew and Aramaic languages, and guided by ritualistic and theological developments within Judaism. The other, resulting from contact with Greek thought and idiom, continues until it becomes identified with the abstractions of Alexandrian philosophy.

The LXX stands at that point where Greek influence begins to make itself manifest in the Jewish religion. The Seventy, however, were restrained by the need of making a faithful translation, and thus did not consistently express their anti-anthropomorphic attitude. This tendency nevertheless is strong enough to give to the LXX a unique character and a somewhat different conception of God from that which is found in the Hebrew Old Testament.

[12] Abelson, *Immanence of God, passim;* Schechter, *Aspects, passim;* Moore, " Christian Writers on Judaism," *HTR*, XIV, pp. 197-254.

APPENDIX I

During the course of this investigation definite evidence has been
found that B is more anti-anthropomorphic than A. This is a textual
matter which raises serious questions as to the nature of these two
texts. A in many passages " exhibits a text which has been systemati-
cally corrected so as to agree more closely with the Hebrew." [1] B is
regarded as for the most part presenting a text which is relatively
close to the LXX in its oldest form; yet every passage must be considered on its own merits. Questions, however, arise in this connection.
Is the reading of B or of A nearer the original LXX in these cases?
How shall we account for these variations? . The examples themselves
must be noted before answers can be given to these queries.

Ex. 9: 29   אפרש את־כפי אל־י״
       (I will spread abroad my hands unto Jehovah);

B   εκπετασω τας χειρας μου
       (I will stretch forth my hands); [2]

A   εκπετασω τας χειρας μου προς τον θεον εις τον ουρανον
       (I will stretch forth my hands to God to heaven);

SH   اهزوهه امـرتا ٍملـ لهءا محزلا
       (I will stretch forth my hands to the Lord).

Ex. 10: 1   אתתי
       (my signs);

B   σημεια
       (signs);

A   σημεια μου
       (my signs);

SH   اثوثا ٍلـ
       (my signs).

[1] Driver, *Samuel*, p. 1.
[2] In Ex. 9: 33 B, however, agrees with the Hebrew:

     και εξετεινεν τας χειρας προς Κυριον
     (and he stretched forth his hands to the Lord).

Ex. 19 : 3   ויקרא אליו י׳׳ מן־ההר

(and Jehovah called unto him out of the mountain) ;

B   και εκαλεσεν αυτον ο θεος εκ του ουρανου

(and God called him from heaven) ;

A   και εκαλεσεν αυτον ο θεος εκ του ορους

(and God called him from the mountain) ;

SH

(and God called to him from the mountain).

Ex. 23 : 28   וגרשה

(and it shall drive out) ;

B   και εκβαλεις

(and thou [Israel] shalt drive out) ;

A   και εκβαλω

(and I [Jehovah] shall drive out) ;

SH

(and they drove out).

Ex. 25 : 2   ויקחו־לי

(that they take for me) ;

B   λαβετε

(take) ;

A   λαβετε μοι

(take for me) ;

SH

(take for me).

Ex. 33 : 15   אם־אין פניך הלכים

(if thy presence go not [with me]) ;

B   Ει μη αυτος συ πορευη

(If thou thyself dost not go) ; [3]

---

[3] In Ex. 33 : 16 B, however, agrees with the Hebrew:

αλλ᾽ η συμπορευομενου σου μεθ᾽ ημων

(except that thou goest with us).

A   Ει μη συ αυτος συμπορευση μεθ᾽ ημων

(If thou thyself shalt not proceed with us);

SH   ܐܢ ܐܢܬ ܠܐ ܐܙܠ ܐܢܬ ܥܡܢ

(If thou dost not go thyself with us).

Dt. 2:22   עשה

(he [Jehovah] did);

B & C-B   εποιησαν

(they did);

A   εποιησεν

(he [Jehovah] did).

Dt. 4:36   השמיעך

(he [Jehovah] made thee to hear);

B & C-B   ακουστη εγενετο η φωνη αυτου

(his voice became audible);

A   ακουστην σοι εποιησεν την φωνην αυτου

(he made his voice audible to you).

Dt. 10:2   אכתב

(I [Jehovah] will write);

B & C-B   γραψεις

(you will write);

A   γραψω

(I [Jehovah] will write).

Dt. 14:22(23)   ואכלת לפני י״ אלהיך

(and thou shalt eat before Jehovah thy God);

B   και φαγη αυτο

(and thou shalt eat this);[4]

A   και φαγη αυτο εναντι Κυριου του θεου σου

(and thou shalt eat this before the Lord thy God).

---

[4] In Dt. 14:25(26), however, B agrees with the Hebrew:

και φαγη εκει εναντιον Κυριου του θεου σου

(and thou shalt eat there before the Lord thy God).

Dt. 32:41   למשנאי

                   ([to] them that hate me);

B   τοις μισουσιν

                   (them [dat.] that hate);

A   τοις μισουσιν με

                   (them [dat.] that hate me).

From these examples certain observations can be made. First, in every example, i. e., that part of the example which is directly connected with the problem at hand, except two (Ex. 23:28 and 33:15), A agrees with **M**, and in these two cases, A is even more anthropomorphic than the Hebrew. This agreement of A with **M** coincides with the general character of Λ as noted above. Secondly, since the Syro-Hexaplar has no asterisks in these examples, to indicate an addition from the Hebrew text which was not in the original LXX, it probably means that A represents in these cases a recension made in pre-Origenian times; but the evidence is not conclusive.[5] Thirdly, where these passages are extant in the Chester Beatty papyri, they always agree with the reading of B, which points quite conclusively to the closer proximity of B to the original LXX than A.

It is quite natural, therefore, that A, which usually follows the Masoretic text more closely, should have more anthropomorphisms than B. B, on the other hand, with its usually shorter text, shows the anti-anthropomorphic tendency more clearly than A.

[5] There undoubtedly were pre-recensional adaptations of the LXX to a Hebrew text before Origen and perhaps even before Aquila, Symmachus and Theodotion. On the other hand the lack of diacritical marks in the SH may be the result of the transmission of an imperfect fifth column of the Hexapla, or they may have been lost in the transmission of the SH itself. See Gehman, "The Relations between the Hebrew Text of Ezekiel and that of the John H. Scheide Papyri," *JAOS*, LVIII, pp. 92-102; "Relations between the Text of the John H. Scheide Papyri and that of the other Greek Mss. of Ezekiel," *JBL*, LVII, pp. 281-287; *Scheide-Ezekiel*, pp. 73-79. Grossouw, *Coptic Versions*, pp. 08 ff.; review, Gehman, *JBL*, LIX, pp. 531-534.

APPENDIX II

ANTI-ANTHROPOMORPHISMS IN AQUILA, SYMMACHUS AND
THEODOTION

The purpose of this study is to see how Aquila, Symmachus and
Theodotion rendered the anthropomorphic passages of the Hebrew
text in comparison with the LXX translation, as well as to see how
they differed amongst themselves in regard to this anti-anthropomorphic tendency. The examples were gathered from the extant
material found in Field's *Hexapla* and the third group of footnotes
in the " Larger Cambridge Septuagint " edited by Brooke and McLean.
Since this is not directly connected with our study, but reflects rather
a side issue, an economy of space has been sought. Accordingly, the
passages are merely cited, not quoted, and a brief statement is made
after each one as to the way it compares with the Hebrew or LXX text.
The examples themselves are given in the table on the following page.

The statistics gathered from this study are as follows: out of 31
examples, 'A has 25 agreeing with **M**, i. e., they are not anti-anthropomorphic, 5 which are anti-anthropomorphic, and one which cannot be
classified; out of 32 examples, Σ has 19 agreeing with **M**, i. e., they
are not anti-anthropomorphic, 10 which are anti-anthropomorphic, and
three which cannot be classified; out of 17 examples, Θ has 14 agreeing
with **M**, i. e., they are not anti-anthropomorphic, 2 which are anti-
anthropomorphic, and one which cannot be classified. Amongst themselves, 'A differs from Σ once in having a literal Hebrew translation;
Σ differs from Θ once in having a more refined translation; and 'A
differs from Σ and Θ once in having again a more literal Hebrew
translation.

Thus 'A agrees with **M** more often than do the other two, with the
possible exception of Θ. At least Σ agrees with **M** least often. Therefore Σ has more anti-anthropomorphisms than the other two, which
is what one expects from the nature of the translations.[1]

---

[1] Swete, *Introduction*, p. 53.

71

AQUILA

Gen. 5: 22 (agrees with M)
"   5: 24 ("   "   ")
"   6: 6a ("   "   ")
"   6: 6b ("   "   LXX)
"   6: 7 ("   "   M)
"   6: 9 ("   "   ")

"   18: 30 ("   "   ")
"   32: 30(31) (agrees with M)

"   50: 19 (agrees with M)

Ex. 1: 21 (agrees with M)
"   3: 14 ("   "   ")
"   4: 12 ("   "   LXX)
"   4: 15 ("   "   ")
"   4: 24 ("   "   M)
"   5: 3 ("   "   ")
"   17: 6 ("   "   ")
"   19: 22 ("   "   ")
"   21: 6 ("   "   ")
"   24: 10 ("   "   ")
"   24: 16 ("   "   ")
"   25: 7(8) (" "   ")
"   25: 29 ("   "   ")
"   31: 17 ("   "   ")
"   33: 15 ("   "   ")

Lev. 24: 15 (agrees with M)
"   24: 16 ("   "   LXX)

Dt. 3: 26 (dif. from M & LXX)
"   4: 36 (agrees with M)
"   9: 7 ("   "   ")
"   9: 25 ("   "   ")

"   32: 10 ("   "   ")

"   32: 4, 15, 31 (dif. from M & LXX)

SYMMACHUS

Gen. 1: 27 (dif. from M & LXX)
"   5: 22 (agrees with M)
"   5: 24 ("   "   ")
"   6: 6a (απεστρεψεν)
"   6: 6b (επεπεσεν)

"   8: 21 (renders meaning of M; not like LXX)
"   15: 1 (dif. from M & LXX)
"   18: 25a & b (renders meaning of M; not like LXX)

"   32: 30(31) (transliteration)
"   41: 16 (agrees with M)
"   50: 19 ("   "   ")

Ex. 1: 21 (agrees with M)
"   4: 12 ("   "   LXX)
"   4: 15 ("   "   ")
"   4: 24 ("   "   M)
"   5: 3 ("   "   LXX)
"   17: 6 ("   "   M)
"   19: 22 (dif. from M & LXX)
"   21: 6 (agrees with M)
"   24: 10 (dif. from M & LXX)
"   24: 16 (agrees with M)
"   25: 7(8) (" "   ")
"   25: 29 (dif. from M & LXX)

"   33: 15 (agrees with M)

Lev. 24: 15 (agrees with M)

Num. 1: 53 (agrees with M)
"   23: 19 ("   "   LXX)

Dt. 9: 7 (agrees with M)

"   9: 24 ("   "   ")
"   32: 10 ("   "   ")
"   33: 27 ("   "   ")

"   32: 31 (dif. from M & LXX)

THEODOTION

Gen. 6: 9 (agrees with M)
"   8: 21 ("   "   ")

Ex. 3: 14 (agrees with M)

"   4: 24 ("   "   ")
"   5: 3 ("   "   LXX)
"   17: 6 ("   "   M)
"   19: 22 (dif. from M & LXX)

"   25: 7(8) (agrees with M)
"   25: 29 (dif. from M & LXX)

"   33: 15 (agrees with M)

Num. 1: 53 (agrees with M)

Dt. 3: 26 (dif. from M & LXX)
"   4: 36 (agrees with M)

"   9: 24 ("   "   ")
"   32: 10 ("   "   ")
"   33: 27 ("   "   ")
"   32: 4, 15, 31 (dif. from M & LXX)

BIBLIOGRAPHY

TEXTS

Kittel, R., Kahle, P., Alt, A., Eissfeldt, O., *Biblia Hebraica*, editio tertia, Stuttgartiae, 1937.

Walton, B., *Biblia Sacra Polyglotta*, Londini, 1655-57.

Brooke, A. E., and McLean, N., *The Old Testament in Greek*, Cambridge, 1906-.

Rahlfs, A., *Septuaginta, id est Vetus Testamentum Graece Iuxta LXX Interpretes*, Stuttgart, 1935.

Swete, H. B., *The Old Testament in Greek according to the Septuagint*, Cambridge, 1896-1909.

Kenyon, F. G., *The Chester Beatty Biblical Papyri; Descriptions and Texts of Twelve Manuscripts on Papyrus of the Greek Bible*, Fasc. V, *Numbers and Deuteronomy*, Text, London, 1935.

Sabatier, P., *Bibliorum Sacrorum Latinae Versiones Antiquae, seu Vetus Italica*, Remis, 1743.

Ceriani, A. M., *Monumenta Sacra et Profana ex Codicibus Praesertim Bibliothecae Ambrosianae*, V. II, *Pentateuchi Syro-Hexaplaris quae supersunt cum notis. Accedunt nonnulla alia fragmenta Syriaca*, Mediolani, 1863.

Field, F., *Origenis Hexaplorum quae supersunt, sive Veterum Interpretum Graecorum in totum Veterum Testamentum fragmenta*, Oxonii, 1875.

Holmes, R., and Parsons, J., *Vetus Testamentum graecum cum variis lectionibus*, Oxonii, 1798-1827.

DICTIONARIES AND CONCORDANCES

Gesenius, W.,–Buhl, F., *Hebräisches und Aramäisches Handwörterbuch über das Alte Testament*, 17 Aufl. Leipzig, 1921.

König, E., *Hebräisches und Aramäisches Wörterbuch zum Alten Testament*, Leipzig, 1910.

Brown, F., Driver, S. R., Briggs, C. A., *A Hebrew and English Lexicon of the Old Testament*, Boston, 1906.

Bauer, W., *Griechisch-Deutsches Wörterbuch zu den Schriften des Neuen Testaments*, 3 Aufl. Berlin, 1937.

Kittel, G., *Theologisches Wörterbuch zum Neuen Testament*, Stuttgart, 1933-.

Liddell, H. G., and Scott, R., *A Greek-English Lexicon*, A New Edition, Oxford, 1925-40.

Jastrow, M., *A Dictionary of the Targumim, the Talmud Babli and Yerushalmi, and the Midrashic Literature*, London, 1903.

Hatch, E., and Redpath, H. A., *A Concordance to the Septuagint and the other Greek Versions of the Old Testament*, Oxford, 1897-1906.

COMMENTARIES

Cambridge Bible for Schools and Colleges, ed. A. F. Kirkpatrick, Cambridge.
  The Book of Exodus, S. R. Driver, 1911.
  The Book of Deuteronomy, G. A. Smith, 1918.

Delitzsch, F., *A New Commentary on Genesis*, trans. Sophia Taylor, Edinburgh, 1899.
Handkommentar zum Alten Testament, hrsg. W. Nowack, Göttingen.
  Genesis, H. Gunkel, 1901.
  Exodus-Leviticus-Numeri, B. Bäntsch, 1903.
  Deuteronomium und Josua, C. Steuernagel, 1900.
International Critical Commentary, ed. C. A. Briggs, S. R. Driver, A. Plummer, New York.
  A Critical and Exegetical Commentary on Genesis, J. Skinner, 1917.
  A Critical and Exegetical Commentary on Numbers, G. B. Gray, 1903.
  A Critical and Exegetical Commentary on Deuteronomy, S. R. Driver, 1895.
Kommentar zum Alten Testament, ed. E. Sellin.
  Das Deuteronomium, E. König, Leipzig, 1917.
Kommentar zum Neuen Testament aus Talmud und Midrasch, H. L. Strack und P. Billerbeck.
  Das Evangelium nach Markus, Lukas und Johannes und die Apostelgeschichte erläutert aus Talmud und Midrasch, H. L. Strack und P. Billerbeck, Bd. 2, München, 1924.
Kurzer Hand-Kommentar zum Alten Testament, hrsg. K. Marti, Freiburg i. B.
  Genesis, H. Holzinger, 1898.
  Exodus, H. Holzinger, 1900.
  Leviticus, A. Bertholet, 1901.
  Numeri, H. Holzinger, 1903.
  Deuteronomium, A. Bertholet, 1899.
Kurzgefasster Kommentar zu den heiligen Schriften, hrsg. H. Strack und O. Zöckler, München.
  Die Bücher Genesis, Exodus, Leviticus und Numeri, H. Strack, 1894.
  Das Deuteronomium und die Bücher Josua und Richter, S. Oettli, 1893.
Kurzgefasstes exegetisches Handbuch zum Alten Testament, Leipzig.
  Die Genesis, A. Dillmann, 6 Aufl. 1892.
  Die Bücher Exodus und Leviticus, A. Dillmann, 3 Aufl. 1897.

OLD TESTAMENT INTRODUCTION AND THEOLOGY

Abelson, J., *The Immanence of God in Rabbinical Literature*, London, 1912.
Albright, W. F., "The Names 'Shaddai' and 'Abram'," *Journal of Biblical Literature*, LIV, 1935, pp. 173-204.
Ausführliches Lexicon der Griechischen und Römischen Mythologie, ed. W. H. Roscher, Leipzig, 1897-1902.
Baudissin, W. W. G., "'Gott schauen' in der alttestamentlichen Religion," *Archiv für Religionswissenschaft*, XVIII, 1915, pp. 173-239.
Bois, H., *Essai sur les Origines de la Philosophie Judeo-Alexandrine*, Paris, 1890.
Bousset, D. W., *Die Religion des Judentums*, Berlin, 1903.
Box, G. H., "The Idea of Intermediation in Jewish Theology," *Jewish Quarterly Review*, XXIII, 1932-3, pp. 103-119.
Dalman, G., *Der Gottesname Adonaj und seine Geschichte*, Berlin, 1889.
  Die Worte Jesu, 2 Aufl. Leipzig, 1930.

Davidson, A. B., *The Theology of the Old Testament*, New York, 1914.

Dhorme, R. P., " L' Emploi Métaphorique des Noms de Parties du Corps en Hébreu et en Akkadien," *Revue Biblique*, XVII, 1920, pp. 465-506; XVIII, 1921, pp. 374-399, 517-540; XIX, 1922, pp. 215-233, 489-517; XX, 1923, pp. 185-212.

Driver, S. R., *An Introduction to the Literature of the Old Testament*, New York, 1913.

Notes on the Hebrew Text and the Topography of the Books of Samuel, 2nd ed. Oxford, 1913.

Drummond, J., *Philo Judaeus*, London, 1888.

Eichrodt, W., *Theologie des Alten Testaments*, Leipzig, 1933-9.

Ewald, H., *Old and New Testament Theology*, trans. T. Goadby, Edinburgh, 1888.

Fairweather, W., *The Background of the Gospels*, Edinburgh, 1908.

Geiger, A., *Urschrift und Übersetzungen der Bibel*, Breslau, 1857.

Giesebrecht, F., *Die alttestamentliche Schätzung des Gottesnamens*, Königsberg, 1901.

Ginsburg, C. D., *Introduction to the Massoretico-Critical Edition of the Hebrew Bible*, London, 1897.

Ginzberg, L., " Anthropomorphism and Anthropopathism," *The Jewish Encyclopaedia*, New York, 1901.

Goodhart, H. L. and Goodenough, E. R., *The Politics of Philo Judaeus*, New Haven, 1938.

Gordon, C., " אלהים in its Reputed Meaning of ' Rulers, Judges '," *Journal of Biblical Literature*, LIV, 1935, pp. 139-144.

Grether, O., *Name und Wort Gottes im Alten Testament*, Giessen, 1934. (Beihefte zur Zeitschrift für die alttestamentliche Wissenschaft, 64.)

Heinisch, P., *Griechische Philosophie und Altes Testament*, II *Septuaginta und Buch der Weisheit*, Münster i. Westf., 1914. (Biblische Zeitfragen, 7 Fol., H. 3.)

Hempel, J., *Gott und Mensch im Alten Testament*, Stuttgart, 1936.

Husik, I., *A History of Medieval Jewish Philosophy*, New York, 1916.

Kohler, K., *Jewish Theology*, New York, 1928.

Köhler, L., *Theologie des Alten Testaments*, Tübingen, 1936.

Lagrange, M. J., *Le Judaïsme*, Paris, 1931.

Leisegang, J., " Indices ad Philonis Alexandrini Opera," *Philonis Alexandrini Opera quae Supersunt*, hrsg. L. Cohn und P. Wendland, Bd. 7, Berolini, 1930.

Marmorstein, A., *The Old Rabbinic Doctrine of God*,
I *The Names and Attributes of God*, Oxford, 1927.
II *Essays in Anthropomorphism*, Oxford, 1937.

Marti, K., *Geschichte der Israelitischen Religion*, Strassburg, 1903.

Montefiore, C. G., *The Old Testament and After*, London, 1923.

Montgomery, J. A., " ' The Place ' as an Appellation of Deity," *Journal of Biblical Literature*, XXIV, 1905, pp. 17-26.

Moore, G. F., " Christian Writers on Judaism," *Harvard Theological Review*, XIV, 1921, pp. 197-254.

"Intermediaries in Jewish Theology," *Harvard Theological Review*, XV, 1922, pp. 41-85.

Judaism, V. I, Cambridge, 1927.

Morgenstern, J., "Biblical Theophanies," *Zeitschrift für Assyriologie*, XXV, 1911, pp. 139-193; XXVIII, 1914, pp. 15-60.

Oehler, G. F., *Theology of the Old Testament*, trans. G. E. Day, 9th ed. New York, 1885.

Pfeiffer, R. H., "Hebrews and Greeks before Alexander," *Journal of Biblical Literature*, LVI, 1937, pp. 91-100.

Introduction to the Old Testament, New York, 1941.

Schechter, S., *Some Aspects of Rabbinic Theology*, New York, 1909.

Schürer, D. E., *Geschichte des Jüdischen Volkes im Zeitalter Jesu Christi*, 4 Aufl. Leipzig, 1909.

Sellin, E., *Alttestamentliche Theologie*, Leipzig, 1933.

Siegfried, C., *Philo von Alexandria*, Jena, 1875.

Weber, F., *Jüdische Theologie auf Grund des Talmud und verwandter Schriften*, Leipzig, 1897.

Wendland, P., *Die Hellenistisch-Römische Kultur in ihren Beziehungen zu Judentum und Christentum*, Bd. 1: 2, Tübingen, 1912.

Die Urchristlichen Literaturformen, Bd. 1: 3, Tübingen, 1912. (*Handbuch zum Neuen Testament*, hrsg. H. Lietzmann.)

Zorell, F., "Der Gottesname ' Šaddai ' in den alten Übersetzungen," *Biblica*, 8, 1927, pp. 215-219.

SEPTUAGINT STUDIES

Baudissin, W. W. G., *Kyrios als Gottesname im Judentum und seine Stelle in der Religionsgeschichte*, hrsg. O. Eissfeldt, Giessen, 1929.

Bertram, G., "Der Begriff 'Religion' in der Septuaginta," *Zeitschrift der deutschen morgenländischen Gesellschaft*, NF, XII, 1933, pp. 1-5.

"Der Sprachschatz der Septuaginta und der des hebräischen Alten Testaments," *Zeitschrift für die Alttestamentliche Wissenschaft*, NF, XVI, 1939, pp. 85-101.

Dähne, A. F., *Geschichtliche Darstellung der jüdisch-alexandrinischen Religions-Philosophie*, Halle, 1834.

Deissmann, G. A., *Bible Studies*, trans. A. Grieve, Edinburgh, 1901.

Die Hellenisierung des Semitischen Monotheismus, Leipzig, 1903. (Sonderabdruck aus den "Neuen Jahrbüchern für das klassische Altertum, Geschichte und deutsche Literatur," 1903, pp. 161-177.)

Frankel, Z., *Vorstudien der Septuaginta*, Leipzig, 1841.

Über den Einfluss der palästinischen Exegese auf die alexandrinische Hermeneutik, Leipzig, 1851.

Freudental, J., "Are there Traces of Greek Philosophy in the Septuagint?", *Jewish Quarterly Review*, II, 1890, pp. 205-222.

Gehman, H. S., "The Relations between the Hebrew Text of Ezekiel and that of the John H. Scheide Papyri," *Journal of the American Oriental Society*, LVIII, 1938, pp. 92-102.

"Relations between the Text of the John H. Scheide Papyri and that of the other Greek Mss. of Ezekiel," *Journal of Biblical Literature*, LVII, 1938, pp. 281-287.

Gfrörer, A. F., *Kritische Geschichte des Urchristenthums.* I Theil, *Philo und die jüdisch-alexandrinische Theosophie*, Stuttgart, 1835.

Grossouw, W., *The Coptic Versions of the Minor Prophets—a Contribution to the Study of the Septuagint*, Rome, 1938. (Monumenta Biblica et Ecclesiastica, 3.)

Hatch, E., *Essays in Biblical Greek*, Oxford, 1889.

Johannessohn, M., *Der Gebrauch der Präpositionen in der Septuaginta*, Berlin, 1925. (Nachrichten von der Gesellschaft der Wissenschaften zu Göttingen. Philologisch-Historische Klasse, 1925, Beiheft.)

Johnson, A. C., Gehman, H. S., Kase, E. H., Jr., *The John H. Scheide Biblical Papyri—Ezekiel*, Princeton, 1938.

Johnson, S. E., "The Septuagint of the New Testament," *Journal of Biblical Literature*, LVI, 1937, pp. 331-345.

Meecham, H. G., *The Letter of Aristeas*, Manchester, 1935.

Swete, H. B., *An Introduction to the Old Testament in Greek*, Cambridge, 1900.

Thackeray, H. St. J., *A Grammar of the Old Testament in Greek*, V. I, Cambridge, 1909.

Thackeray, H. St. J., *The Septuagint and Jewish Worship. A Study in Origins*, London, 1921.

INDEX OF BIBLICAL PASSAGES

(Figures in parentheses refer to the Hebrew text.)

GPSR Authorized Representative: Easy Access System Europe - Mustamäe tee 50, 10621 Tallinn, Estonia, gpsr.requests@easproject.com

www.ingramcontent.com/pod-product-compliance
Ingram Content Group UK Ltd.
Pitfield, Milton Keynes, MK11 3LW, UK
UKHW021826290326
469463UK00006B/254